Treasured Moments

Compiled and Edited by
Yvonne Lehman and Terri Kalfas

GRACE

Broken Arrow, OK

Scripture quotations marked ESV are taken from *The Holy Bible, English Standard Version*. ESV® Text Edition: 2016. Copyright © 2001 by Crossway Bibles, a publishing ministry of Good News Publishers. Used by permission. All rights reserved.

Scripture quotations marked KJV are taken from the *King James Version* of the Bible.

Scripture quotations marked NIV are taken from *The Holy Bible, New International Version*®, NIV® Copyright ©1973, 1978, 1984, 2011 by Biblica, Inc.® Used by permission. All rights reserved worldwide.

Scripture references marked NLT are taken from *Holy Bible, New Living Translation*, copyright © 1996, 2004, 2015 by Tyndale House Foundation. Used by permission of Tyndale House Publishers, Inc., Carol Stream, Illinois 60188. All rights reserved. Used by permission.

Royalties for this book are donated to Samaritan's Purse.

TREASURED MOMENTS

ISBN-13: 978-1-60495-097-7

Copyright © 2024 by Grace Publishing House. Published in the U.S.A. by Grace Publishing House. All rights reserved. No part of this book may be reproduced in any form or by any electronic or mechanical means, including information storage and retrieval systems, without permission in writing, except as provided by U.S.A. Copyright law.

From Samaritan's Purse

We so appreciate your donating royalties from the sale of the books in the *Divine Moments* series to Samaritan's Purse.

What a blessing that you would think of us! Thank you for your willingness to bless others and bring glory to God through your literary talents. Grace and peace to you.

Our Mission Statement

Samaritan's Purse, a nondenominational evangelical Christian organization provides spiritual and physical aid to hurting people around the world.

Since 1970, Samaritan's Purse has helped victims of war, poverty, natural disasters, disease, and famine with the purpose of sharing God's love through His Son, Jesus Christ.

Go and do likewise.
Luke 10:37

You can learn more by visiting our website at
samaritanspurse.org

Dedicated to Yvonne Lehman and the many authors who have so generously contributed their stories to all of the books in the *Divine Moments* series.

Contents

INTRODUCTION 7
1. *A Special Delivery Package* ~ Robert B. Robeson 8
2. *My Favorite Color* ~ Tanja Dufrene 14
3. *Louis Vuitton* ~ Carol Graham 16
4. *Tea and Leaves* ~ Janet Faye Mueller 19
5. *Walking the Aisle with Mom* ~ Norma C. Mezoe 21
6. *A Fetching Feast* ~ Annmarie B. Tait 23
7. *Holy and Tuesday* ~ Lola Di Giulio De Maci 28
8. *Is That Our Baby?* ~ Diana Derringer 31
9. *Mom's Holding Faith* ~ Norma C. Mezoe 33
10. *My Birthing Story* ~ Vera Brennan 36
11. *The Summer I Time Traveled* ~ Charles J. Huff 39
12. *Go Ye!* ~ Ben Cooper 44
13. *Never So Thrilled to See a Toilet* ~ Vicki H. Moss 48
14. *Self-Portrait as an Opera Girl* ~ Laura Sweeney 51
15. *God's Lullaby* ~ Lydia E. Harris 54
16. *You Only Get So Many Memorable Moments* ~
    Robert B. Robeson 56
17. *Supermen and Superwomen* ~ Bob LaForge 63
18. *Beauty from Ashes* ~ Norma C. Mezoe 65
19. *Fried Green Tomatoes and Me* ~ Nanette Thorsen-Snipes 67
20. *The Great Hunter* ~ Helen L. Hoover 70
21. *Pajama Party for Two* ~ Lisa Braxton 72
22. *Snapshots of a Childhood Summer* ~ Diana Derringer 76
23. *The Moments I Didn't Pass Up* ~ Tammie Edington Shaw 77
24. *The Philly Ice Cream Parlor* ~ Lola Di Giulio De Maci 79

25. *Twice Owned* ~ Janet Faye Mueller 82
26. *Derby Day* ~ Annmarie B. Tait 84
27. *The Sparrow May Fall* ~ Carol Graham 89
28. *Playhouse* ~ Beverly Hill McKinney 92
29. *Crochet* ~ Amari Seymour 95
30. *Working for My Good* ~ Norma C. Mezoe 96
31. *War Dogs* ~ Robert B. Robeson 100
32. *In Memory of Dazzle* ~ Lola Di Giulio De Maci 105
33. *Mom's Never-Failing Gift* ~ Diana Derringer 108
34. *Singing Songs of Love* ~ Terri Elders 111
35. *About Winter* ~ Sue Rice 115
36. *Popsicles Can Have Names* ~ Melissa Henderson 116
37. *Come What May* ~ Vicki H. Moss 120
38. *Abiding* ~ Nanette Thorsen-Snipes 125
39. *Goin' ta Jesus* ~ Mary Anne Quinn 128
40. *At the Restaurant* ~ Tim O'Keefe 132
41. *Nutting* ~ Janet Faye Mueller 135
42. *The Well-Watered Plant* ~ Lin Daniels 137
43. *You've Been Here a Long Time* ~ Melissa Henderson 139
44. *Dear Denise* ~ Robert B. Robeson 141
45. *Porches and Swings, and Treasured Moments* ~ Terri Kalfas ... 145

ABOUT THE AUTHORS 149

Introduction

This book began as an idea from Yvonne Lehman. She had just started to gather stories before her death in 2021.

I had met Yvonne several years earlier, when she invited me to be on the faculty of The Blue Ridge Mountains Christian Writer's conference, which she founded and led until she retired after twenty-five years.

Yvonne was the type of person who wanted to make sure those attending her conferences went away with many treasured moments . . . and usually, information overload.

My favorite memory of her at a conference was when, in her early 70s, she made her entrance into the auditorium and onto the stage for the first evening session riding behind a local law enforcement officer on his motorcycle . . . dressed just as you might imagine.

Although no story in this book is about Yvonne or anyone's experience at a writers conference, the Divine Moments series came to be because she approached me about publishing one book and I replied, "Why not an entire series?" Thus began the journey of writers sharing stories of special moments of various types.

I hope the stories you read here bring to mind your own treasured moments. And maybe, just maybe it will encourage you to jot them down for future generations to enjoy.

Terri Kalfas

~ 1 ~

A Special Delivery Package

Robert B. Robeson

May 9, 1970. Another oppressively hot and humid Asian afternoon was drawing to a close for our helicopter medical evacuation crew of four near Da Nang, South Vietnam. I was a pilot and commander of the 236th Medical Detachment (Helicopter Ambulance) located at Red Beach on the southern shore of Da Nang Harbor.

My medic for the day was 1st Lt. Ron Reidenbaugh, a close friend who also functioned as my administrative medical officer on the ground. "The Mauler," a nickname I'd tagged him with because of his size and aggressive outlook on life, was a young man you liked right away — perpetually smiling and always full of humor. At six feet two inches and two-hundred-thirty-five muscular pounds, he was an imposing figure who'd been a defensive end in football at Kent State University before being commissioned as an officer.

In the previous month, the thirteen pilots in our unit had experienced having sixteen helicopters shot up or shot down. We'd gone through our authorized inventory of six helicopters nearly three times. Because our crews had been stretched to the maximum, Mauler had volunteered to fly as a medic (due to his extensive medical training at Kent State) to give a few of our enlisted medics a breather.

We had just completed a number of difficult medical evacuations of wounded South Vietnamese soldiers from remote jungle locations. Now we were lifting off from our field-site aid station at Landing Zone Hawk Hill to fly two ambulatory patients and a youthful, pregnant Vietnamese woman on a litter to the Vietnamese hospital in Da Nang, approximately thirty-six miles away.

A few minutes after takeoff, a call came over our FM radio. We were asked to evacuate an Australian civilian from the coastal town of Hoi An. His ankle had been crushed by a heavy fifty-gallon drum. We made the pickup en route and flew north along the South China Sea toward Da Nang.

After the second takeoff, Mauler noticed our pregnant patient was beginning to stir. Her eyes had been closed. Now she was alert and the old mama-san accompanying her was pointing and attempting to communicate in high-pitched Vietnamese.

"I think the aid station was a bit off on its estimate," Mauler said. "Doc told me she wasn't going to deliver for a couple of days." He had a rare frown on his face. "Can you go any faster? I've never delivered a baby before."

I turned in my armored seat and glanced at the fragile-looking young woman lying on a litter covered with yesterday's bloodstains. We were at two thousand feet with the cargo doors open. Her long black hair was blowing in the refreshing slipstream. Her black peasant garments were tucked in at the waist and knotted.

"Can you go any faster?" Mauler repeated. "She's in labor."

"It's redlined," I replied.

Silhouetted against the light green of the South China Sea, behind and far below, Mauler bent hunchbacked beside her litter.

Our rotor blades beat against the air and wore down the minutes as I initiated a rapid descent and approached the triple peaks of Marble Mountain marking the southeastern outskirts of Da Nang.

Normally, all Vietnamese patients were taken to the Vietnamese Province Hospital in the center of Da Nang. But, as aircraft commander, I'd already made the decision to take her directly to the U.S. Army 95th Evacuation Hospital located on China Beach next to the South China Sea. Here she would get the best and quickest medical care available.

"We're not going to make it," Mauler said matter-of-factly over the intercom.

"I'll call ahead and have a nurse standing by on the pad at the 95th," I said.

Everyone in the aircraft was suddenly concerned for this mother-to-be and the tiny life about to be born into a war zone. Glancing over my shoulder, I was amazed to see that her face was not distorted by pain. Instead, it held a peacefulness not often observed by soldiers accustomed to the danger, devastation, and death of everyday combat situations.

The next words I heard, coming a short time later, were those of our crew chief. "Congratulations, sir. We've got us a girl!"

When I turned around to see, Mauler's hands were covered with blood. He was cradling a tiny infant.

Those arms that had effortlessly knocked two-hundred-pound men around on the gridiron now tenderly held this small child. We all heard the first sharp wail of life above the roar of our rotors and Lycoming jet engine.

I thought back to other days, to previous moments — mystical moments — when we'd rescued someone from under enemy fire whom we'd been seeking for a long time. I experienced now what I'd felt then . . . reverence. Suddenly it hits you and you discover in an instant awareness of how wonderful a human life is, no matter where in the world it's located.

An American nurse met the aircraft as we scattered a group of medics playing volleyball not far from the concrete landing pad. As her gurney passed them, these medics moved closer and seemed to sense what was written on everyone's faces. For this distinct moment in time, at least, we were a part of *life*. Then, without any coaching or explanation, they began to applaud the young woman, her newborn, and their bulky escort.

I caught the young mother's eye as her gurney passed my cockpit window and made a circle with my thumb and forefinger. She reacted to this international sign with a shy smile and slight wave of a thin hand.

After shutting down at our airfield, Mauler walked the eighth of a mile to my hootch with me. His war, to that point, had been doing administrative tasks on the ground, and in an office where lives weren't in constant jeopardy. For a few days then, he'd discovered that combat flying could be exciting, dangerous, often fear-filled, yet extremely fulfilling because of the opportunities to impact lives one-on-one.

"For once I feel like I did something worthwhile," Mauler admitted. "It can be a real kick, can't it?"

I nodded my head. After ten months in daily combat — and having flown over nine hundred medical evacuation missions to that point — I understood what he meant. He'd been responsible for preserving the lives of a number of wounded soldiers earlier that morning. Now he'd been intimately involved in welcoming a new traveler onto our spinning ball of clay. That's a good day's work for anyone.

This unique special delivery, when citizens of three different nations cared and shared together for the common good of a new life on this planet, reminded me of another baby born nearly two-thousand years before in Bethlehem. That, too, was a peasant birth that relied on the kindness of strangers during difficult and dangerous moments.

My generation's war has long since been over, but I've often prayed that this baby girl escaped the demise of her country a few years later. Because every child has potential, is important, and we can never predict the impact one specific life will make in our world.

I often replay that mission in my mind. Now I realize it was a victory of life in the midst of death. That baby's birth was a solitary and unique rose that bloomed without fanfare in God's springtime garden in Southeast Asia to provide a sense of hope for us all.

It was a "special delivery" package I doubt any of us will ever forget.

Postscript

In previous wars, crew chiefs of fighter aircraft would take pride in denoting the number of planes shot down by their pilots. The usual method was by painting a small replica of the enemy's flag on the side of the aircraft.

A few days after this flight, I went down to our flight line to preflight my aircraft. On the pilots' doors, on each side of the helicopter, our crew chief had painted his own small symbol: a white stork with a tiny baby suspended in a diaper from the stork's bill. I guess he felt it was important to make a point of keeping score, too.

~ 2 ~

My Favorite Color

Tanja Dufrene

My rather independent four-year-old stood there so proud of herself. She was quite enthusiastic about the outfit she had put together. Taking a quick glance at her from head to toe, I gently encouraged her to consider different shoes and socks. She had selected a lovely purple top embellished with an array of jewel-toned buttons paired with black pull-on pants. Her socks were star-bright yellow. Her ensemble was completed with tennis shoes designed for Christmas celebrations — red and green plaid with metallic gold threads woven throughout.

Unfortunately, that was a time when parents were often shamed for the inconsistent appearances of their children. I struggled to hide the flood of emotions that welled within me. She was growing up fast, and I knew fostering her confidence was important. I was so proud of how she took initiative. Yet we were about to embark on a day full of activities . . . in public! How could I encourage her, yet save both of us from the shame and embarrassment misplaced comments would foster?

Before further objections were made, she announced, "But, mama, *rainbow* is my favorite color to wear!" Stunned, I simply had no words. To this day I can still hear how she emphasized the word so dramatically. Her spirited resistance made me giggle, melting my resolve and concern — and continues to bring a smile to my face. Though her choice of attire that day was initially troubling, I continue to find inspiration in it, especially when I read these words:

Since God chose you to be the holy people he loves, you must clothe yourselves with tenderhearted mercy, kindness, humility, gentleness, and patience. Colossians 3:12 NLT

There it was — the ultimate goal of how we should dress ourselves for interaction with one another. Rather than limiting our concern solely about our outward appearances, as we dress our bodies for the events of each new day, we should consider how we will clothe our minds, our hearts, our souls, and our attitudes, for these will outshine whatever covers our bodies.

Eventually I came to realize that what one might see as a mismatched four-year-old's outfit, another might see as a lovely array of colors bursting with youthful delight on a tenderhearted child full of kindness.

May we, too, see the same in those around us.

~ 3 ~
Louis Vuitton

Carol Graham

It was our first evening dogsitting while our teenage daughter was on vacation in Costa Rica for two weeks. In vain, Louie, aka Louis Vuitton, searched the entire house for his "mommy." Then, that disappointed but determined Miniature Dachshund formulated a plan.

While my husband, Paul, and I were watching TV, we heard a commotion on the stairs leading to Rochelle's bedroom on the third floor. Something heavy was being dragged down the stairs, causing a loud thumping sound. I peeked around the corner and saw the six-month-old puppy laboriously dragging his large, hard-sided Louis Vuitton carrier down the staircase.

He glanced at us, wagged his tail, and scurried back upstairs.

"What do you think he's doing?" my husband asked.

We watched in amazement as Louie dragged his worldly possessions, one by one, down those stairs: first, his blankie, then his bowl, bone, ball, and sweater. He even made one last trip to get his leash.

The project took most of the evening, and Louie never tired. He was on a mission, but we were not certain what it was . . . yet.

Louie had put thought and reasoning into each move. He

took each of the personal items he had lugged down the stairs and put it in the carrier. It was extremely difficult because the carrier had a lip that was considerably taller than he was.

After Louie finished packing his "suitcase," he attempted to jump inside. It took several tries before he made it. But he wasn't done yet. Once inside, he got the zipper between his teeth and, with all the strength he could muster, he pulled the zipper closed. I envied his patience and tenacity.

Then he lay down and went to sleep.

The message was abundantly clear. He wanted to go see his mommy. He had seen her pack her suitcase and go away. He must do the same so he could find her. He stayed in the carrier all night, and when I unzipped it in the morning, he was elated. Believing he had arrived, he jumped up — but Mommy was not there.

I started making notes about Louie's escapades to share with Rochelle. He surprised us with new undertakings every day.

When the telephone rang, he would run to it, knock it off the hook and bark until we picked up the receiver and said, "Hello."

His absolute favorite activity was going for a car ride. The possibility of stopping at McDonald's for chicken nuggets was his inducement.

But one day, my husband didn't stop at McDonald's and then left Louie in the car with the window cracked while he went off to do an errand. That dog, with legs about two inches long, managed to jump out the window of Paul's truck and land without injury. He then walked two blocks in a busy urban area and found Paul in a hardware store. As Paul was paying for his purchase, he heard a man say, "Well, little fellow, where did you come from?"

Paul was shocked to look down and find Louie, who looked up at him as if to say, "Here I am. I found you all by myself. I waited at the streetlights with all the other people. Aren't you proud of me? Can we have chicken nuggets now?"

Indeed, they stopped for some nuggets on the way home.

One evening, when I put Louie outside to pee, I noticed a huge black bear in the driveway. I screamed at Louie to come back inside the house. Instead, he fearlessly charged the bear's back legs and nipped at them. The bear ran as fast as he could to get away from the annoying little dog. I was terrified yet laughing hysterically at Louie's bravado.

For Christmas that year, I turned Louie's daily journal into a hardbound book written from a dog's perspective. When Rochelle opened her gift, she laughed and cried at the same time.

I will never forget her words: "Mom, *now* will you write your memoir?" She began a campaign, and no matter what excuse I gave her, she persisted until I finally said, "Yes!"

Writing Louie's story changed my life, and set me on the path to a new career as an author and radio talk-show host. Louie is an old, gray-haired dog now — just as cute, certainly as smart, and still up to his old — and new — tricks.

~ 4 ~
Tea and Leaves

Janet Faye Mueller

I sit at my writing desk looking out over the fields yellowed and browned with age and listen to the farmers' machinery humming in the distance. Once again, I am overwhelmed with the golden warmth of this season. The sweet scent of earth and ripe fruit, described by poet John Keats as "mellow fruitfulness," hangs in the air. A few oak leaves flutter and twist their way to the ground, and suddenly mixed in are heavy drops of rain, first a few, then more and more as the storm picks up volume and speed.

I quickly get up to close the sliding doors and at once the house is quiet. Dusk begins to settle in upon our little villa, and I decide to abandon my desk in honor of my nightly autumn ritual. I lift the silver teapot off its place on the nearby coffee bar and fill it with cold water. Before long, she is chattering away on the stovetop, her voice rising higher and higher to a fever pitch, letting me know it is time. Craving something sweet, I choose a dessert tea, Candied Chestnut, described on the box as having sweet, light chestnut notes and a smooth buttery finish. That should do. Soon my senses are filled with chestnuts and memories, and with tiny, careful steps so as not to spill a drop, I make my way back to my desk.

Feeling chilled, I grab a trusty, plaid blanket lying close by and wrap my shoulders tightly. Settling in once again, I sip the hot brew and nod self-approvingly on my selection tonight.

Pulling an oak leaf from the dried floral arrangement on my desk, I study it thoughtfully. When I rake them, these sturdy leaves don't crush and break as easily as the maple and ash. Like the tree itself, they silently boast of strength and durability.

"It's been a hard season, this season of the pandemic," I murmur to myself. I twist the leaf by its stem and watch it twirl in my hand. The words to a song echo through my mind, and I join in, quietly singing to the leaf, the tea, and myself. "You never know just what tomorrow holds, and you're stronger than you know, oh, you're stronger than you know."

And at this precise moment, I know I have everything I need.

~ 5 ~
Walking the Aisle with Mom

Norma C. Mezoe

When I was very small, a caring woman took me to Sunday school and worship services.

As I became an older child and then a teenager, I walked to a church in my neighborhood. I attended alone because my parents were not Christians.

At fifteen, I was being led by God's Holy Spirit to accept Jesus Christ, but I was too shy to walk the aisle by myself to make that decision public.

When a revival was beginning at the church I attended, the minister stopped at our house to invite Mom. She was hesitant at first, but eventually promised the minister she would attend.

The first night of the revival, Mom and I sat close to the door because it would be convenient in case we wanted to leave. However, we stayed. On the second night, as the congregation sang "Softly and Tenderly," Mom told me she was going forward.

Her heart had been touched to accept Jesus Christ. I wanted to go too, but that long aisle ahead seemed to stretch forever. I tried to talk Mom into waiting until the final verse, but she wouldn't wait. So, I walked the aisle with her, and we made our decisions known.

Mom's road as a Christian wasn't smooth because my father wouldn't attend services and he denied God's existence. Still, for as long as she was physically able, Mom faithfully attended.

I know I would have had the courage to walk that long aisle alone eventually, but with Mom at my side, I was encouraged to do so earlier rather than later.

Perhaps, through the years I attended church alone, God's Spirit was speaking to Mom about salvation. Whatever the cause behind it, I am thankful she heard and obeyed.

I will never forget the happy memory of walking the aisle with her.

Many times, through the witness of a family member's faith in God, an entire family will be led to accept salvation.

If you struggle to live your faith before an unbelieving family, don't give up. God may use your witness to bring about their salvation.

~ 6 ~
A Fetching Feast

Annmarie B. Tait

I'd planned our menu in my head for six months. That's how long it took before Joe asked me out after we'd met. And by the looks of the things you'd have thought I'd spent the entire six months cooking. You couldn't wedge a toothpick between the stuffed celery, fried chicken, deviled eggs, potato salad, pickled beets, ham sandwiches, macaroni salad, crisp veggie sticks, buttermilk biscuits, carrot salad, ripe red strawberries, or the glistening green grapes crammed into the basket. In fact, I had to put the dessert — brownies, chocolate chip cookies, and snickerdoodles — into a separate basket!

Dad eyed my colossal assortment as Joe was pulling into our driveway.

"A watermelon might round things out, but he's driving a Pinto. As it is, you're already going to have to borrow my roof rack."

"Oh Daddy, We will not!"

"If this spread doesn't hook him, nothing will."

"It's just a date, Dad. I'm not trying to hook anybody."

"Yeah, okay. I've seen your first dates before. This is a hook!"

"Shhh! He'll hear you!"

The bell rang and Daddy swung open the door. Joe stepped up and shook his hand.

"You must be Mr. Tait. It's very nice to meet you."

"I am," Dad said. "Come on in. I hope you're hungry."

"Okay Daddy, that's enough out of you." I said.

Joe looked over at me and smiled in a way that assured me my choice of a white sundress splashed in multi-colored polka dots had been a good one. He looked rugged in his Kelly-green polo shirt and slightly-faded blue jeans that complemented his hazel eyes and sun-bleached hair.

I smiled in return. This casual look proved much more inviting than seeing him across the lunch table in a boring shirt and tie. We'd spent six months doing that.

I pointed to the picnic hamper. "Joe if you'll get the food we'll be on our way."

Daddy laughed. "Did you bring a fork lift, Joe?"

Joe's eyes widened. Okay, it was an oversized, wicker laundry basket with a red-checkered table cloth draped over the top and tucked in around the sides.

"Wow! Who else is going on this picnic?"

"Um, nobody," I said, discreetly slipping the basket of desserts behind me.

"Wow! I should have skipped eating . . . this week."

He stifled a groan as he lifted the laundry basket and headed out the door. "We'd better shove off. I'll need the rest of the day to put a dent in this."

I scooted out the door in front of Joe then hurried over to the car. Oh no! The Pinto only had two doors. What if we couldn't squeeze the mega basket into the back seat?

Joe must have read the panic on my face.

"Relax, Annie. It's a hatchback," he said as the hatch popped open and he deposited the basket.

"Phew!" He sighed feigning exhaustion as he opened the passenger door. I slipped into the front seat and rested the basket of baked goodies on my lap.

"That's a purse right? You couldn't possibly have more food in there."

I shrugged and smiled. "I guess you'll have to wait and see."

Church bells chimed noon as we started out. I figured we'd arrive at the lake in about a half hour. The map was clear and X's marked the spots where we'd need to turn.

I'd been there before so don't ask me what went wrong, but at the half-hour mark I realized I had no idea where we were.

As the clock approached 1:15, I'd lost all confidence in my map reading and was staring out the window feeling foolish and stifling tears of embarrassment.

"Annie, are you sure you've been here before? You seem lost."

"Well," I said, "I have been here before but I've never driven here myself. I guess that makes all the difference."

"Uh huh," Joe said. "Do you mind if I take a look at the map? This is the third time we've passed St. Michael's Church."

By now it was 1:45. Joe reached across and pulled the map from the top of the dessert basket.

With a double fudge brownie in one hand and the map in the other, he noshed and studied.

Of course Joe had to show off by using all kinds of technical terms like "east" and "west," but he eventually determined we were only about five miles from our destination and merely had to turn around and head west.

"We're closing in on the place, Annie. I can feel it. I need to make a u-turn here and turn right at the next intersection. According to the map it's only five miles down the road. I'm starving!"

My cheeks grew scarlet as my eyes welled with tears once again. "I'm sorry, Joe. If I'd just given you the map in the first place we'd have arrived long ago."

"What? Annie, I'm not complaining. I'm just thinking if the brownie I just ate is any inkling of what's waiting for me in the laundry basket, I'm going to need until sundown to get through it and I don't intend to miss anything."

As Joe predicted, we rolled up to the lake in just a few minutes. Once we chose a spot I plucked the red-checkered cloth from the top of the laundry basket with a flourish, laid it on the grass and arranged the smorgasbord.

True to his word, Joe spent the rest of the afternoon sampling every dish. It was going on five o'clock when he dabbed his mouth with a paper napkin then fell back onto the grass, and groaned.

"Annie, I think I may explode. But what a way to go!"

We walked hand in hand along the lake for another hour watching the golden sun begin it's decent on the horizon of the crystal blue lake.

I knew even on that first date that he was my one and only.

Four years later, on the day we were married, Daddy looked at Joe and said, "Annie's my little girl Joe. Take good care of her."

"Oh I will," Joe replied. "I've been *hooked* on Annie since I all but sprained my back carrying that picnic basket."

With an arched eyebrow Daddy cast a glance in my direction and chuckled.

Upon arriving home from our honeymoon Joe found a copy of *Field and Stream* stuffed in our mailbox.

"I wonder where this came from," Joe said.

With my own eyebrow arched, I cast a glance in his direction and chuckled.

"I think Dad's trying to tell me I'm a heck of a fisherman."

~ 7 ~
Holy and Tuesday

Lola Di Giulio De Maci

For weeks before Easter Sunday 2022, I watched closely as a mother Canada goose sat gingerly on top of her unhatched eggs, waiting patiently for the arrival of her baby goslings. Every so often she would stand up and rotate her body, then sit back down on her eggs in a new position. I had the perfect vantage point for the upcoming births, as my second-floor apartment's window overlooked the facility's garage roof where the miracle would take place.

There's a pond nearby where Canada (not Canadian) geese and other birds make their home year round. I call watching their antics my "reality TV." Seagulls, swans, egrets, ducks, crows, cranes, and a lone owl gather in the neighborhood with a cacophony of sounds that create their own symphonic masterpiece. I'm never bored.

With their black necks extended several inches in front of their brown bodies, the Canada geese are the most outstanding in this orchestrated performance, honking annoyingly loud to let you know they are flying by. At times they fly in a V-formation.

Night after night I sat by my window with my gaze constantly on the top of the garage roof where the blessed event would take place. Occasionally two black crows would dive-bomb the expectant mother getting close enough to make me want to yell out the window, "Stay away from her!"

I don't know how she staved them off. But she did.

After what seemed like an eternity and a day, the father goose arrived and proudly perched himself on the highest point of the garage roof as if he were on security patrol.

"Something's about to happen," I told myself. "Something very important." I could feel it. I learned that once the mother has laid all her eggs, the eggs are incubated for approximately twenty-eight days. Anywhere from two to twelve eggs can be hatched, but the usual number is five.

Finally, after holding a vigil the entire time mother goose was nesting, I had the honor to witness two adorable baby goslings hatch. They resembled the fuzzy yellow chicks that appear at Eastertime. And coincidentally, this was Holy Tuesday — the Tuesday before Easter Sunday. So, proudly taking it upon myself to be their honorary godmother, I named one gosling Holy and the other Tuesday.

Leading his new family in procession, the father goose paraded all around the roof, the mother behind him and the goslings following their mother. Once the march was completed, the father and mother left the roof and landed on the ground below, leaving the goslings alone to fend for themselves.

"Now what?" I wondered. I thought the parents would carry their babies on their backs to the ground. Or they would all fly down together. Or . . . .

What I learned was that newborn goslings cannot fly until

they are about three months old. So, they jump down to the ground — from up to three stories high — and land unharmed.

Once the goslings were on the ground, the family of four waddled away to their new home as if on an afternoon stroll.

Holy and Tuesday stayed with Mother Goose and Father Goose about one year before they went out on their own. Then they were able to "leave the nest" and fly away, testing their newfound independence!

I felt so honored and privileged to have witnessed the ever-unfolding, incredible mystery of creation that has taken place since the beginning of time.

The amazing, unbelievable miracle of new life is truly a gift.

~ 8 ~

Is That Our Baby?

Diana Derringer

Cast all your anxiety on him because he cares for you.

1 Peter 5:7 NIV

"Crystal's in the hospital. They have to take the baby."

"Both were in respiratory distress. A helicopter took Kaleb to Lexington."

"Something's wrong with Crystal's heart. Without immediate surgery, she won't live."

Two days sped by in a blur of phone calls, rapidly-worsening circumstances, hospital transfers, and medical jargon. The wife of my nephew, Trevor, struggled for her life following an emergency Caesarean section one night and open-heart surgery the next. A heart pump kept her alive.

Their son, Kaleb, born seven weeks early, lay in a neonatal intensive care unit eighty miles away. With tiny arms thrown to each side, his almost lifeless body rarely moved. We were told that if he survived, lack of oxygen before birth could cause significant physical and mental problems. Realizing the gravity of their situation, friends and family around the world prayed.

My nephew and his in-laws stayed with Crystal. Kaleb's

grandmother Gail and I stayed with Kaleb. After a physically and emotionally exhausting day, Gail and I poured out our hearts for Crystal's future and the weight on Trevor's shoulders. Then we prayed for Kaleb: "Lord, make him a fighter. Help him cry and work his little lungs. Let him get mad and throw those arms and legs around."

The next morning when we entered the neonatal ICU, we froze, totally confused. I double-checked the nametag over Kaleb's bed. My sister actually asked a nurse, "Is that our baby?"

The incubator and respirator were gone. Waving his arms and legs, Kaleb was wailing like a siren! He had the most beautiful little temper tantrum we had ever witnessed. Tears flowed as Gail held him, fed him, sang to him, and told him how much his mommy and daddy loved him and couldn't wait to be home with him.

He went home in only ten days. His parents joined him after one month, minus the heart pump. Miracle followed miracle, but that first one left us no doubt that God hears the specific desires of our hearts.

What burdens your heart today?

Give it to God.

Whatever the outcome of your current struggle, God promises His never-failing presence and love.

~ 9 ~
Mom's Holding Faith

Norma C. Mezoe

"Is your mother going to come after you?" The words surprised me, but I quickly recovered. "No, I have my own car," I replied. I was cleaning my parents' house and it was my mother who had asked the question.

I had suspected Mom's problem was more serious than the small strokes and Parkinson's that had been the doctor's diagnosis. Some time before, Mom had left a note on my front door. The words had been scrambled and senseless.

As the dementia worsened, Mom sometimes became more agitated at night. One night Dad phoned, asking for help because she would not go to bed. When I arrived, she told me, "Mom and Pop just live up the road. I want to go visit them tonight."

Of course, her parents had died many years before. I was finally able to calm her by promising she could visit her parents the next morning.

The years passed, and at the age of eighty-one, Mom was only a shadow of her former self. She was able to eat without assistance, but caregivers met most of her needs.

Then Dad needed surgery, so while he was in the hospital, I stayed with Mom in the evenings. After working at my job, I stopped at home to gather clothing for the next day and then I spent the night with Mom.

One evening as I walked into their house she asked, "Where are the others?" She thought people were coming to eat with her so she had fried several chicken legs for the occasion. Thankfully, she had turned off the stove burners. Once before, Dad had come home to discover all of the burners on the gas stove turned on.

Mom was a Christian. Before the illnesses she had consistently read her Bible and attended worship services at her church. Now she made no attempt to read the Bible and she never mentioned her church. That bothered me. I yearned for assurance that she was still holding on to her faith.

Each night after taking care of Mom's needs, I pulled the covers down on her bed and tucked her in as she had done with me when I was a young child. Turning back the hands of time, I told her good night the way she had done with me all of those long-ago years, "Nighty-night."

She looked up at me, smiled, and repeated, "Nighty-night."

That ritual went on for several nights. Then one bedtime, as I stood ready to say good night, Mom reached up and grasped my hands. Words began tumbling from her mouth. At first, I didn't understand what she was mumbling. Looking down, I discovered her eyes were closed. She wasn't talking to me — she was praying! I heard her conclude with "and Lord, help us all to be better Christians."

My concern had been needless. Mom was holding tightly to her faith in Jesus Christ. I whispered, "Nighty-night," kissed her on the forehead, and tiptoed from her room.

I had been given my assurance. I had known all along that the Lord would never forget or forsake Mom, but it was such a blessing to know that under the blanket of confusion in her mind, her faith was still holding.

~ 10 ~
My Birthing Story

Vera Brennan

As we ladies gathered around the mom-to-be, the hostess announced, "Let's share with Jane our birthing stories!" Eyes glance nervously in my direction. Nearly everyone knew I was childless; in fact, I had just entered menopause.

As I waited my turn, trying to figure out what to share, I remembered those long-ago days of hope — *Maybe this time* — only to be disappointed month after month. At age 27, I could no longer handle the ache; I screamed out to God. "If I'm not going to have children, I'd rather be dead!"

God had answered by pointing me to Philippians 4:11-13, the verse in Scripture where Paul wrote he had learned to be content whether in want or plenty. I'd questioned that. Could I learn to be content with or without a baby to cuddle? Yet here I was twenty years later, still quite alive, and actually content.

Finally, my turn to share came. I could feel all eyes on me, tension filling the room. Then in that moment, God reminded me, and I began to tell *my* birthing story.

Rainey and Pete lived upstairs in the building where I worked. One day, a very pregnant Rainey invited me to have lunch with her in their apartment.

As I bit into my sandwich, she asked, "Vera, how come you never had kids?"

"Well, it wasn't because I didn't want them," I spluttered. "But God in His goodness taught me how to be content and when my marriage ended in divorce, I was actually grateful! My parents were divorced and I didn't want to put my kids through that."

She looked at me sympathetically and then, with a glint in her eyes asked, "Would you like to see what it's all about?"

"What do you mean?"

"Come watch the birth of this baby." She rubbed her stomach. This wasn't her first child.

"Is that allowed?"

"Sure! I'm going to deliver at the Northern Dutchess Birthing Center. It'll be all natural. You'll get to see the real thing!"

Who could pass up an offer like that? It was arranged; Pete would contact me when Rainey went into labor.

However, when the call came, I was at a conference in New Hampshire, a good five-hour drive away.

I was torn. I hesitated. Though the evening session of the conference had just finished, my car was back at the hotel. Plus, it would mean driving back to New York in the middle of the night alone! But Pete had said, "If you want to see this baby born, you better leave now!"

Around 4 A.M., I climbed the stairs to my apartment and called Pete, only to learn that the contractions had ceased. Rainey was at home. Not sure what this meant, I left on my clothes and laid down on the couch with the phone beside me.

It did not ring all that day or the next.

Then, almost forty-eight hours after I had left the conference, the call came.

I walked into the birthing room. They greeted me: Rainy in position; Pete at her side. This was Rainey's fifth baby. She knew how to give birth. No moans, no screams, just a quiet, "I don't think I can do this" before the final push.

Out popped Leanne's head! With her eyes wide-open — so alert, so alive — she looked all around, checking out this new world into which she had just arrived.

I was stunned. I had never realized that a baby already had a mind of its own before it left the womb. The enormity of it overwhelmed me.

But then followed the afterbirth! That overwhelmed me even more. My stomach churned; my legs grew week. I headed for the door and squatted down (a trick I had learned) — before I fainted!

"And that, ladies, is *my* birthing story!" Everyone laughed. The tension had dissipated. I knew once again, that the Lord had indeed met me that long-ago morning through His Word just as He had tonight by giving me "*My* Birthing Story."

~ 11 ~
The Summer I Time Traveled

Charles J. Huff

When I was around twelve years old, I took a trip back in time. Back to a time with no electricity, and no indoor plumbing. A time of kerosene lamps, wood cook stoves, feather beds, and iceboxes. A time of scythes and sickles, and drawing water from a well with a rope and bucket.

My time portal was my grandparents' old home place. The trip taught me a lesson for a lifetime.

Each spring, Grandpa and Grandma would get a family member to drive them from Decatur to their old home place near the small town of Omega, Illinois, where they spent the summer. There they would plant a garden, harvest wild fruit and berries, and preserve all they gathered for winter food in Decatur.

Before any of the gardening could happen, Grandpa and Grandma had to get the place ready to live in for the summer.

In 1962 we took them.

Upon arrival, the first step was to move a section of the barbed-wire fence back against the fencerow. A grassy lane between the field and fencerow provided access to the field and the old house that sat about a quarter mile from the country road. Grass and wildflowers had already grown about knee high around the house.

Grandma and Grandpa, Mom and Dad set about unloading the car. They had packed everything from the Decatur home they would need for the summer, including their victuals (vittles, as they called them).

Grandma busied herself cleaning the house and putting things away. Grandpa prepared his tools for cutting down the tall grass the next day, giving help to Grandma when she needed it.

It didn't matter who took them; each summer the routine was always the same. While Grandma and Grandpa were busy setting their things in order, someone (this time Mom and I) drove back to Omega to buy a thirty-pound block of ice to put in the icebox.

All I remember of Omega is a gas station/grocery store and a post office. The town may have had more buildings than that, but the grocery store where we bought the block of ice is all that remains with me.

Until the produce they grew started coming in, the icebox kept milk, butter, and eggs cool. As the harvest of vegetables and berries filled the icebox, store-bought items like the milk, eggs, and butter, were kept from spoiling by putting them in a bucket and lowering it into the cool well water. When a sufficient quantity of produce had been accumulated, Grandma canned the vegetables and fruit, making some of the fruit and berries into jam or jelly.

When I was dropped off to spend a week with them, I was surprised to find the yard had been mowed and neatly manicured. Grandma explained that the first thing Grandpa had done was take a scythe and sickle to the tall grass and then cut it down to normal yard grass with a manual push mower.

As one might expect, for a boy who grew up with the TV there was little to do there for just entertainment's sake. However, there was one "yard toy" I will always remember. It was simply a wagon wheel on an axle that protruded out of the ground at an angle. Grandpa taught me to stand on the lower rim of the wheel with at least two rungs between my feet, and grasp the top of the rim with two or three rungs between my hands.

"Now shift your weight to one side and then the other as the wheel turns back."

It was the same principle used to get a swing to reach greater heights. After enough times, the wheel would spin all the way around, turning me head down and up again, round and round. I spent a lot of my time on it.

When night came, Grandma or Grandpa lit the kerosene lamps. Those provided a weak yellow light in the room and cast shadows of everything around us. Grandma used the light to set things back in order after dinner, giving the morning a fresh start. To me, the dim light and shadows seemed perfect for campfire ghost stories, but the familiarity of the lamp's glow never triggered such thoughts for Grandma and Grandpa. To conserve fuel they let the lamps burn for only a short time. Afterward, we would either end up outside sitting and talking, or we would go to bed early.

The best part of going to bed was getting into the feather bed Grandma had fluffed up full from the night before. Lying back felt like I was doing a backstroke on a cloud.

Take a new pillow, fluff it up and then lay your head on it. Feel it puff up around your head, caressing your ears and face.

Now imagine that over your whole body. One couldn't help but have sweet dreams on it.

In my short lifetime, I had already heard Grandpa's hunting stories so many times I could recite them to him. Visiting them in Decatur always brought a sense of dread, because I knew I would have to listen to them again. However, at the farm all those hunting stories sprang to life as Grandpa told them. I felt like I was preparing to go with him on the night-hunt for hawks, sensing the desperation of making sure we killed both the male and the female in the nest.

One night my imagination was piqued by that morning's sighting of timber wolf tracks, which triggered a story I had not heard before. Maybe living in surroundings of a bygone era heightened my imagination and caused emotions to surface as Grandpa lamented over times past. I cannot explain it, but in that moment I was living inside Grandpa's memories. The sights, sounds, smells and tension became real to me.

We lingered on the porch that night, looking up at millions of stars and enjoying the cool of the evening. As it was getting close to time to go to bed, Grandpa spoke about how many nights the family would start a fire to sit around outside and the whippoorwills would come close and sing. In the moonlight tears glistened in his eyes as he said he wished the whippoorwills would come back so he could hear them again.

It brought tears my eyes, too. They had not gone; they were nearby and were calling, but his aged ears could not hear them. I couldn't tell him. Instead, I left him alone in his reverie and learned to appreciate the friendship of the whippoorwills for myself.

Many summers have come and gone since that summer, and with them Grandma and Grandpa and even Mom, Dad, and my brother have slipped away. I now live where there are no whippoorwills. My wife, kids, and grandkids haven't heard their friendly song.

Like Grandpa, I feel like nothing can compare to listening to the song of the whippoorwill under a starlit sky with those you love.

~ 12 ~

Go Ye!

Ben Cooper

Guest speakers for when the pastor is away can remind me of a substitute teacher in school. You really don't know what to expect until you hear them. I have been on both sides of that equation. Nevertheless one Sunday evening, when a guest speaker shared about some of his short-term mission trips to various countries, I was captivated. Growing up in the church had allowed me to hear countless others share similar stories. But on this night, something was different.

The speaker talked of places he had been, but he also mentioned a place where he was planning to go. It was a small island named St. Lucia in the British West Indies. Quite frankly, I don't think I had ever heard of it prior to him bringing it up. But for some unexplained reason, it grabbed my attention. Little did I know at the time that God was hatching a series of favorite moments for me.

After the service, I questioned the speaker about the trip and took his prayer card. I couldn't explain it, but I had an unexpected urge to be part of that trip. God didn't audibly speak to me, but the Holy Spirit compelled me to go. I was a husband and father of young children; it didn't make sense to those around me when

I began making plans. I will say my wife was onboard with my decision. We left the financing for the two-week trip in God's hands. As we watched, He covered the entire cost.

The primary focus was to host a teen camp for the island. We rented a school for a week and welcomed eighty teenagers to camp. Our team consisted of eight adults and four teenagers. Each day included Bible lessons and fun activities. Evenings were reserved for services that presented the salvation message.

On Tuesday night, the lead missionary gave a clear challenge and several teens responded. I walked up to one fourteen-year-old boy and prayed with him as he accepted Jesus into his heart. I gave him a Bible and spent time with him each day to help him grow as a new believer.

When I left at the end of the two weeks, the Holy Spirit gave me the feeling that I would be back. I was. I returned to help out with camp two years later, and again the following year. God impressed upon me to go, and He always provided the finances.

At the conclusion of my third trip, having logged a total of six weeks getting to know people from St. Lucia, I no longer felt the need to return. But God dishing out favorite moments was far from over.

Over the years, I kept in contact, by way of snail mail — it took two weeks for a letter to be delivered — with the young boy I met the first year. Now he was heading off to Bible college in Puerto Rico. He had begun a habit of calling me on Christmas Day every year and did so his first year in college. I asked him what his plans were for the summer. When he said he didn't really having any, I felt compelled to ask if he would be interested in coming to the States to work at a summer Bible camp. He agreed and I made the arrangements. He spent seven summers with us as he went through college and graduate school. He quickly became part of the family and got to see my five children grow up.

While he attended graduate school in Michigan, he met a wonderful young woman and proposed to her. When she said "yes," he called me to tell me the news and ask if I would be his best man in the wedding. He also asked if he could list my wife and me as his parents. We were honored and agreed.

As their children started coming on the scene, he would call and tell me about the next one due. When he called to let me know that they were expecting their fifth child, I asked, "How many are you planning on having?" His reply was, "Five, just like you, sir!"

Today he is serving as pastor of a church in Oklahoma and teaches at a nearby Christian school. We rarely get to see him and his family, but we still enjoy getting phone calls and seeing how quickly his children are growing up.

What a marvelous journey this has been because I was compelled to "Go!" on a short-term mission trip to an island in the Caribbean! That decision turned into a lifetime of treasured moments. I was obedient and gained a son-in-the-faith and his family. It is amazing to think that years ago I answered the call to go to another country and share the precious Gospel with teenagers. In doing so, it generated a desire for that young man to come to the United States to share the Gospel message with campers. And now he is preaching it in the church God has called him to serve. I am thankful for all the divine and favorable moments He has provided because I followed His command in Matthew: "Go Ye!"

> *"Go ye therefore, and teach all nations, baptizing them in the name of the Father, and the Son, and of the Holy Ghost."*
>
> Matthew 28:19 KJV

~ 13 ~
Never So Thrilled to See a Toilet

Vicki H. Moss

I thought I'd had it with toilets. I have a love/hate relationship with them. Always looking for one when out in public and always repairing one in private. Almost every single one of my "thrones" has eventually leaked or overflowed, or had "the whine" — that sound one makes when the bobber thingie in the tank won't float to the top, causing excessive water bills because the water runs nonstop. Throughout the years, I've had so many potties fixed and even though I know toilets are a necessity, to think about them wore me out.

Until something big happened from the ancient world. Here's the story.

I never thought I'd live to see the day that I'd be thrilled to see an old toilet turn up. But when archaeologists announced in 2017 they had discovered a toilet during a dig in the ancient town of Lachish, located southwest of Jerusalem, I happy-danced through my house. Because this wasn't just any old commode. This was the toilet referred to in 2 Kings 10:27: *They demolished the sacred stone of Baal and tore down the temple of Baal, and people have used it for a latrine to this day.* This toilet was placed there by King Jehu for a reason. And the truth was finally made known: He really did destroy idols and turn Lachish into a latrine as the Bible claims.

But let me share the background to this story. After Jehu, commander of fellow officers, was anointed king of Israel by a man from the company of the prophets through instructions given by the prophet Elisha, the same man gave Jehu a message from God as he poured the oil on Jehu's head:

> *"This is what the LORD, the God of Israel, says: 'I anoint you king over the LORD's people Israel. You are to destroy the house of Ahab your master, and I will avenge the blood of my servants the prophets and the blood of all the Lord's servants shed by Jezebel. The whole house of Ahab will perish. I will cut off from Ahab every last male in Israel–slave or free. I will make the house of Ahab like the house of Jeroboam son of Nebat and like the house of Baasha son of Ahijah. As for Jezebel, dogs will devour her on the plot of ground at Jezreel, and no one will bury her.'"* 2 Kings 9:6-10 NIV

From this ancient biblical account, we know God was serious about His instructions that no one should worship idols, and His commandment: *Thou shalt have no other gods before me* (Exodus 2:3). So He anointed Jehu, whose name means "God is He," as king to usurp the throne of king Ahab who — along with his wife Jezebel who practiced sorcery and witchcraft — had been worshipping the false god Baal.

After reading about that ancient find, I began to think how it seemed God had a funny sense of bathroom humor — at least when he was fed up with disobeying humans. Whatever the case, I now love talking about toilets, at least that one found in Israel.

And when I tell people about the commode that's been uncovered from antiquity, I also tell them about another thing I've discovered from modern times: Universal toilet guts do not fit inside every brand. So don't be fooled when it comes to idol worshipping or the intricacies of toilet guts. They're both something you don't play around with because there are repercussions with either one.

I hope this bit of news has been a blast from the past, and will also give you something new to think about when visiting your own home throne. Much better than thinking about that chain you will have to rehook because, for some reason, they always slip through the tiniest gap in the little triangle you have to fish for when the toilet won't flush.

The good news is, when we get to heaven we will be made perfect. (I hope that means we'll also no longer need a commode.) The only thrones we'll see will be the ones where God is seated along with His One and Only at His right hand.

Thank you, Jesus!

~ 14 ~

Self-Portrait as an Opera Girl

Laura Sweeney

I enter the Blank Center for the Performing Arts accompanied by Jaime Reyes, owner of Montebello Bed & Breakfast, the site of my current writing workshop.

Jaime is several years my senior, retired from a career as a Department of Transportation civil engineer. Opera is his hobby. He built the local guild from nothing.

Last night we attended *La Comte Ory*, the skill of Bel Canto. "It's farcical. 'Opera de bouffe,' opera of buffoons," Jaime had told me. Then he convinced me to return tonight for the deeper message in Verdi. *La Traviata* is Violetta's opera, he explained, about a fallen woman. Not to be missed.

In the summers as I grew up, I attended Indianola's National Balloon Classic, after opera season. Oliver Darling, a couple of grades ahead of me, made All State Vocal Chorus. He studied opera here, at Simpson College. I chose St. Olaf near Minneapolis. Opera was not my forté.

"Are you in love with words?" Jaime asks.

"Not words. Expression," I say. "If I were a painter, I'd love painting, not the paints."

"That's how I approach opera," he says, then remarks about

the woman with a yellow ribbon in her white hair: "An entertainer in Europe during the war," he says, "for the soldiers."

I try to imagine the European librettists and composers as we enter the studio, sit in the front row. "Never sit in the back. Life chooses the ones in front," Jaime says.

The moderator acknowledges the audience. True fans. Groupies. It is Fourth of July weekend. I wonder if I'm the youngest person here.

"It's amazing," Jaime says. "They open their mouths and out flows this sound. So effortless."

"Not effortless." I say. "Years of practice." Then turn to the singer behind me to thank her for last night's solo.

As a teaching artist, I understand the road life, living out of a suitcase. To survive financially, opera artists need a couple of gigs each season. Book in Palm Beach, or wherever, thrive on adoration and accolades, scrub floors to make ends meet. And when they finally make it . . . criticism for wearing gaudy earrings.

The rehearsal starts. White figures float across the stage as the national anthem plays. Throughout the performance, the tenor is weak. *Given Violetta's death, he should be more gut wrenching*, I think. After all, it was the 1800s. TB and infectious death were rampant.

Still, I'm enchanted, but can't help wondering, *Is opera any more relevant in this culture than poetry?*

After the performance, Jaime says, "Shadow me, as a summer project. Witness the training of the stars of tomorrow."

He tells me about an opera-singer friend, a vocal therapist, known for her role in *Tosca*, and suggests I take lessons.

I recall a lesson from a writing conference. One session suggested joining, for a limited time, a group of enthusiasts with whom I wouldn't normally associate. Like people who collect garbage for art. "You need a gatekeeper, inside connections," the instructor said.

Jaime is one of those gatekeepers.

"I'm in," I tell him. Then I commit to attending this season's Des Moines Metro Opera productions — one of America's premier summer festivals — like some people take a good book to the beach.

~ 15 ~
God's Lullaby

Lydia E. Harris

The phone jarred me awake at 2 A.M. "We're going to the hospital!" our daughter announced. "The baby is coming!"

I woke my groggy husband, and we hurried to the hospital. (I don't know why we were in such a hurry because the baby certainly wasn't.) As we waited, we prayed for a healthy child and a safe delivery.

The ultrasound had revealed the gender, but I wanted the official word before announcing our first grandchild. After an eternity of waiting, a blurry-eyed new father came out and announced, "It's a boy! Peter is here."

When I saw our newborn grandson, it was love at first sight. As I cradled him in my arms, I studied the shape of his cute little nose, held his soft tiny hand, and thanked God for Peter Jonathan Faull. God had done it again. He had created another child in His image. "Lord, let him become a child of God too," I whispered in my heart.

After his birth, I delighted just to be with Peter. He didn't need to do anything special — just be himself. If he fussed, I cuddled him and soothed him with love and singing. My tender feelings toward Peter gave me a new understanding of a verse I held dear: *He will take great delight in you. He will quiet you with his love, He will rejoice over you with singing* (Zephaniah 3:17 NIV).

This verse assures me that God cherishes me, calms me with His love, and sings over me with joy. Imagine God feeling that way about you and me!

As my heart overflowed with love for Peter and I treasured spending time with him, I gained a small glimpse of how much God loves me and rejoices over me.

Peter is now a young adult, and I am thankful for the times we share. I pray Zephaniah 3:17 for him and all of our grandchildren: that God will rejoice over them with singing, and that they will awaken each morning secure in our love and the marvelous love of their heavenly Father.

~ 16 ~
You Only Get So Many Memorable Moments

Robert B. Robeson

Every March we see those sixteen-to-eighteen-year-old world-beaters in their Air Jordan's, jocks, and jerseys competing for gold and glory in state high school basketball tournaments around this nation. I still get a thrill observing these kids compete in everything from massive sports arenas with TV coverage, to cracker-box gyms of small town America with only peers and parents watching.

Some of my fondest memories were shared with twelve other guys who earned a trip to the Oregon State High School Basketball Tournament in Eugene in 1960. That year we were 20-2 (tied for the best regular season record of the sixteen teams in Class A competition). To me, the experiences of that season were as rare as live armadillo on a Texas highway.

In 1960, La Grande had a population of barely nine thousand. La Grande High School had a student body of four hundred fifty. This number did not include our ubiquitous and energizing tiger mascot. Our tallest player was only six- feet three inches.

Giving our team a basketball, lighting and heating the gymnasium on those cold December and January evenings, and providing loyal fans — that included a pep band playing "Tiger Rag" — was a little like heaving Bre'r Rabbit into a briar patch. We believed our basketball sanctuary was sacred ground. And we never allowed an opponent to disrespect it by outscoring us. Beating us on our home court that year was about as likely as running into a Spanish matador at our local Dairy Queen. It was akin to Valentino's losing its recipe for pizza. Ain't gonna happen, friend.

I'm at an age now when I'm quick to say, "I remember when," even when nobody is listening. Yet I still savor those hallmark hardwood happenings like dessert from a five-star restaurant. It was a part of American history you won't find in history books . . . only in youthful memories of a select group of today's senior citizens. Those times of sock hops, soda fountains, and Russia's Lunik I and II artificial satellites are as outdated to the young of today as rumble seats and speakeasies were to my generation. Yet all of these "moments to remember" still echo in my mind, like the song with the same name from that era.

Some of the teams we played in those intense high school games were bigger, and even thought they were better, than we were. Only they never made us believe it.

That season, our coach, former U.S. Marine Jack Rainey (now deceased), had a determined mindset to tame and train his young "tigers," rather than take the easy route and paint stripes on a bunch of kitty cats. He always emphasized that if we didn't try we'd never know what we might accomplish. "The simple act of 'trying' shifts your brain into gear and you often get better in spite of yourself."

He used to coax us in practice each day with the same gentle tone an infantry drill instructor uses to suggest a new recruit should "drop" and pump out twenty pushups. We'd rather have breakfasted on road-killed skunk than have been the target of his tart tongue. If you weren't putting out, he could make you feel like you'd just flunked study hall.

Coach made us believe we had a special destiny that year. And, as usual, he was right. Equipped with little more than drive, determination, and dreams, we vacuumed-up the competition from one end of Oregon to the other. He later became assistant athletic director at Oregon State University.

Sometimes, when Coach Rainey wasn't around, we'd plug the drains in our large shower room until the water was three to four inches deep. Then we'd body-surf our bare bones from one end to the other. It was a bit like skinny-dipping in a river or pond in front of an enthusiastic and appreciative audience.

Though my hair is now follically-challenged and I've become part of the bifocal set, I can still recall the distinct "aroma" of wintergreen liniment, Tough Skin, and a locker room filled with sweaty bodies during halftime performance critiques. These were special times I'll always carry with me.

We learned not to let the world limit or dictate to us what we could accomplish in life. We proved the "experts" and prognosticators wrong. We kept our dreams alive and never gave up. Of the twelve young men on that 1960 team, three later earned Ph.D.s and became school principals or administrators. Three became military officers (two of which are now retired colonels who served in combat during the Vietnam War). At least another two earned master degrees. A number of the others graduated from a college/university or completed significant undergraduate study. And one, Rod Chandler, was elected a Republican Congressman from the state of Washington for five terms. I've lost track of the rest and am unaware of what they accomplished in life. But it was probably significant.

As far as Rod is concerned, if you ever run across him say "Hi, Bubbles." That was his nickname. But do yourself a favor. Don't ask him how he got it.

To illustrate how we looked out for each other, I want to highlight how Rod went out of his way to assist me in discovering my destiny. It proves how one act of selfless intervention can change the course of a teammate's life.

Because 1960 was during the military draft era, a few on our squad had already joined our local Oregon Army National Guard infantry unit. Rod was one of them. One day, before our high school graduation, he came by my house to invite me to a Monday night Guard drill so I could see what they had to offer. He mentioned the pay, going to six months of basic training with a group of friends (instead of alone), and not having to face a draft board. After basic, I could return to La Grande and attend Eastern Oregon College in town and fulfill my military obligation without leaving home.

It was much later when someone revealed that Rod had received a five dollar bounty from the unit for recruiting me. Years later, he called me to touch base again after leaving Washington, D.C. I thanked him for introducing me to the military and for the fact I'd been able to make it a twenty-seven-year career —

retiring as a lieutenant colonel after serving on three continents as a medical evacuation helicopter pilot. I also informed him that I'd found out about the bounty. A brief moment of silence ensued. Then he admitted that he "couldn't remember" recruiting me or receiving that money. My next comment was that becoming a politician had probably been the perfect occupation for him.

Rod really had done me a major favor and it's something I haven't forgotten.

A person can never go back to the past but you won't forget most of it either. That's why God gave us memory, so we could have roses in winter and fond recollections of youthful days when we finally enter that crotchety-old-geezer stage of life.

The newspaper clippings from that year are now as yellow as Homecoming mums. I still have the team pass and programs from those games and that state basketball tournament. Whenever I leaf through the pages, it's once again Friday and Saturday night and I can hear "Tiger Rag" blaring in the background . . . making my adrenaline pump and goose bumps appear just as they did then.

A shelf in my home office holds two eight-by-ten photos in ornate sports frames. One is a color photo of our 1960 team after the Redmond game win on our home court, when we qualified for the state tournament. The other is black and white. It shows my father's 1929 Grand Meadow, Iowa High School basketball team. He never made it to State, but he was still able to share a part of this experience with his second son. Born in 1911, he became a Protestant minister and passed on in 2002. One of the things we both learned during those teenage years of athletic competition was that friends and teammates — regardless of race, religion, or relative social class — are truly important in life. We were taught that the only place success comes before work is in a dictionary. We also discovered the value and importance of dedication, discipline, determination, and teamwork.

Memories are not only vehicles to self-understanding, but also ways to reminisce and appreciate the life we've led. For me, the glory days during that 1960 basketball season are now a solitary gleaming jewel whose brilliance is undimmed by over six decades of both radiant and rocky times. It was Camelot and we were King Arthur's knights . . . for a brief duration.

You only get so many memorable moments in life. Those basketball games, in the land and lair of a host of tenacious "tigers," were a few of mine that I'll always treasure.

~ 17 ~
Supermen and Superwomen

Bob LaForge

I often feel I have somehow missed out on something.

I am one of those people who think a lot along the lines of, "What I could do if only I were . . ." If only I were able to write great songs. If only I were able to shoot a basketball with amazing accuracy. If only I had been a famous lawyer . . . or a famous writer . . . or . . . .

Then one day I was watching a Superman movie. Behind the mild-mannered and ordinary Clark Kent was the hero Superman. Clark Kent held a regular job. His clothes were commonplace. His life was nothing extraordinary. He was someone who was like ninety-nine percent of the rest of the population — including me.

But Superman was different. He did great things. What he did made a huge difference. The number of times he saved someone, or even the world, was countless. People pointed at him in amazement and wished they could be like him.

Sort-of like what I thought.

One person but two entirely different worlds.

Which person do I — or any of us — feel more like: Clark Kent or Superman? I am sure that the majority of us feel more like Clark Kent. When we are out in public, no one points at us in amazement. We do not make headlines in newspapers (or the Internet). We are safely in the range of ordinary.

But as born-again Christians, we are actually people who exist in two entirely different worlds. In this world, we are probably pretty ordinary. But in the supernatural realm (*our citizenship is in heaven* — Philippians 3:20 NIV), we are supermen and superwomen. What we do there makes a huge difference to a great many people. We can share the Gospel and someone can go from an eternity in Hell to an eternity in Heaven. That is tremendous! Superman may temporarily save the world from its current near-calamity, but we can be instrumental in saving someone for all eternity.

Or we can pray and something that might seem impossible, or might not normally occur, does happen. It could be a healing, an encouragement, a job opportunity, a reconciliation.

Words we say here, things that we do here, are stored up in heaven where they will never fade away or be destroyed (*store up for yourselves treasures in heaven, where neither moth nor rust destroys, and where thieves do not break in or steal* — Matthew 6:20 NIV). That is far better than being a headliner in a newspaper or on the Internet.

The things we can do as Christians are beyond a superhero's powers. X-ray vision, running fast, flying, superhuman strength. Those are only fiction. Fantasy.

What we can do as Christians is much greater. And it is real! Real people are rescued from the domain of darkness and transferred to the kingdom of God's beloved Son (Colossians 1:13). We are filled with real joy, peace, and hope (Romans 15:13). Real wisdom is given to those who are confused and unsteady (James 1:5). Real angels rejoice when one sinner repents (Luke 15:10).

Maybe that is what Colossians 3:1-2 (ESV) is about: *Therefore, if you have been raised with Christ, keep seeking the things that are above, where Christ is, seated at the right hand of God. Set your minds on the things that are above, not on the things that are on earth.* God does not want us to just walk around on this earth being ordinary. He wants us to set our minds on what is above and look to the supernatural. And as a bonus, He gives us the power of the Holy Spirit (Romans 15:13) to do that and makes all grace overflow to us, so that, always having all sufficiency in everything, we may have an abundance for every good deed (2 Corinthians 9:8).

God wants us to be supernatural supermen and superwomen. When I realized that, it made all the difference.

~ 18 ~

Beauty From Ashes

Norma C. Mezoe

I was fast approaching my 15th birthday when devastating news reached me. The school I attended from first grade had burned down the night before. Nothing was left but charred walls.

When I heard the heartbreaking news, I cried many tears. I was afraid I would be sent to a different school than my classmates because I lived in another town and rode a bus to school.

I was a shy teen and the thought of being forced to attend school with strangers filled me with fear.

So, imagine my joy when I learned only a day before my birthday that all of my high school would be combined with another small school eleven miles from my home! I would still eventually graduate with my classmates.

Those first days in my new school were filled with anxious anticipation, wondering how we would be accepted by the other students. Would they resent our coming and causing confusion and crowding in their school?

My worries were needless. The students and teachers not only accepted us, they went out of their way to help us adjust to the new surroundings.

Out of the ashes of sorrow and anxiety grew a beauty of unity of helpfulness and encouragement between our two schools.

Isaiah 61:3 (NIV) tells us God will *bestow on them a crown of beauty instead of ashes, the oil of gladness instead of mourning and a garment of praise, instead of a spirit of despair.*

When I think about that stressful time, I am reminded that God has been faithful in my past and He will continue to be faithful in my present and in my future. He will work in and through whatever heartache, sorrow, or pain I encounter.

God continues to work to bring beauty from the ashes of my life. He will do the same for everyone who allows Him to guide in their lives.

~ 19 ~
Fried Green Tomatoes and Me

Nanette Thorsen-Snipes

"Mother, how could you!" I opened the screen door of the old clapboard house.

She reached for the cups, then unwrapped newspaper from around a stoneware cup. "This is what your stepfather wanted. He wanted some land so he could have a garden."

My stepfather! He was nothing but a country bumpkin! At fourteen, I was horrified by my mother's marriage to a man from the sticks. To top it off, we'd had to move from the sprawling, busy suburbs to a simple house in the country without so much as a dishwasher — except me.

That first week I barely spoke to my mother, and I pretended my stepfather didn't even exist.

When school was out for break the week of Easter, I was still not on civil terms with my stepfather. I observed his every move with judgmental anger. On Monday of that week, I sat on the back porch steps with my arms folded and watched him shovel dirt into a sunny patch of our back yard.

Later that week, he broke up the red clay and tossed rocks and broken limbs into a nearby ditch. The next day, he added fertilizer to the soil, and then raked until it was smooth.

When Friday arrived, I watched him squint against the sun's glare, his neck and arms reddened from the constant bombardment of rays. In his hand, he held a small plastic bag. Every once in awhile, he'd grab a handful of something, then drop it into the small holes he dug in the dirt.

My curiosity high, I walked over to him, squishing the cool topsoil between my bare toes.

Without a word, my stepfather poured a dozen seeds into my waiting hand. With calloused hands born of a farming life, he dug into the cool soil. Lovingly, he dropped in a couple of seeds, then pushed dirt over them.

To my surprise, I felt my anger begin to dissipate as I followed his example and finished my first row.

Spring gave way to summer, and with it came harvest. I was delighted to find butter-yellow squash hiding beneath dark green leaves. I loved snapping the squash from the vine and putting them in a basket, adding a few cucumbers, and picking pole beans for supper.

When my stepfather suggested I pick the green tomatoes, I was aghast. "They're not red yet."

"Go ahead and pick some," he said, "and I'll show you how to fry them."

Thinking he'd lost his mind, I pulled several of them and added them to my already-full basket.

Inside our small old-fashioned kitchen, my stepfather taught me how to slice the tomatoes, dip them in cornmeal, and fry them in hot oil.

I'll never forget that first sweet bite.

My stepfather also showed God's love. Gradually, he helped me tear down the wall I had built between us. It reminded me of when he'd broken up the soil to prepare it for cucumber seeds.

As a teenager, it wasn't easy trying to care about someone so different from me, especially the man who had taken my father's place. But when I shared in the planting that year, I felt the birth of a seed that blossomed into caring.

And to think, it all began with just one seed.

~ 20 ~
The Great Hunter

Helen L. Hoover

"Oh look, there's a mouse!" Ginger, our nine-year old daughter, exclaimed.

"Where? Do you still see him?" my husband, Larry, asked.

"He's under the chair watching us," six-year-old Grant said.

"Oh no, I'll have to set a trap," I complained.

We had been watching a movie on TV. Larry got up off the couch and said, "Wait, I'll shoot him. You all stay here."

"Shoot him? Here in the house? That's not good," I said as Larry headed to the bedroom where he kept his guns.

"His ears are twitching," Grant noted.

As Larry came back into the room, he announced, "I'll use the BB gun. Is he still there in the corner?"

"Yes!" the three of us answered in unison.

We had a good line of sight across the room, under the wooden rocking chair, and back to the corner where the mouse watched the proceedings.

"You three stay there on the couch and be quiet. Let's not scare him," Larry told us.

Happy to oblige, the three of us pulled our feet up onto the couch to watch.

Larry is a good shot with a gun, so we figured the mouse was a goner. He slowly crawled over in front of the chair and gradually lay down on his stomach so he could look under the chair toward the mouse. He placed the BB gun on the floor, under the rocking chair in front of him.

The mouse hadn't moved.

As Larry sighted down the barrel of the BB gun, with his finger on the trigger, the mouse suddenly sprang onto the barrel of the gun and ran toward him.

Larry scrambled to get up, but with his socks and long pants on, his legs just slid on the floor. With legs and arms flailing in all directions, he was a hilarious sight.

Finally, he scooted back toward the couch and asked, "Did you see where the mouse went?"

"He ran into the hallway as you were panicking on the floor," I informed him.

Larry caught his breath and said, "When the mouse started running toward me on the gun, I had visions of him biting my nose. But I couldn't get any traction to get off the floor."

Giggling uncontrollably, Ginger told him, "Dad, you are 'The Great Hunter'."

The demise of the little mouse came a couple days later, when he was tempted by the peanut butter on the trap I set out.

Over the past fifty years the Great Hunter story has been told and retold at various family gatherings and to friends. It still brings smiles and giggles to those hearing it.

A cheerful heart is good medicine, but a crushed spirit dries up the bones. Proverbs 17:22 (NIV)

~ 21 ~

Pajama Party for Two

Lisa Braxton

My mother attended her first pajama party when she was eighty-three years old. And that was because I decided to host it for her.

As her health began to fail her world became very small. Appointments with the physical therapist who guided her on short walks through the house had been canceled. The nurse's aide who'd gotten her into the shower and then could only give her sponge baths at her bedside had been told not to come back. The prepared dinners from Meals on Wheels were stacked high in the refrigerator and were barely touched.

I packed a couple of suitcases, kissed my husband goodbye and headed out the door after Mom's doctor let us know that there was nothing more to be done to treat the ovarian cancer that had metastasized and was spreading rapidly.

"Make new memories. Enjoy this time," her doctor had said.

I kept that thought in mind during the road trip back home.

One morning, I raised Mom's bed to a sitting position and we watched *The View*, one of her favorite talk shows. She'd always enjoyed the gossip, entertainment news, political banter and clashing barbs among the co-hosts.

It was October 7, 2020. The women were talking excitedly about the vice-presidential debate to be broadcast nationwide that night. Vice-President Mike Pence and Senator Kamala Harris would have their one and only debate before the presidential election on November 3rd.

Excitement had been building in our family for weeks, ever since Harris had been announced as Joe Biden's running mate. Harris was our sorority sister. She, Mom, and I were members of Alpha Kappa Alpha Sorority, Inc., which has a largely African American membership across the United States and other countries. Numbering in the hundreds of thousands of undergraduate and graduate chapter members, the women are committed to service and sisterhood.

As the ladies on *The View* speculated on the Pence-Harris debate and its outcome, I said to Mom, "Let's have a pajama party."

She gave me a weak smile. "How are we going to do that?"

Obviously this would not be a typical pajama party, the kind I had been invited to when I was a little girl, with lots of giggling, pillow fights, and plugging in the E-Z Bake Oven at two in the morning to make a pancake-size German Chocolate cake. This would be an opportunity for Mom and me to have mother-daughter time, knowing our time together would soon come to an end.

"We'll have it right here. I'll take care of everything."

"Okay," she said. Her eyelids fluttered shut as she dozed for a nap.

Preparation would be simple. No food would need to be cooked; no popcorn popped, or bags of chips opened. Mom ate little and took in as much liquid as she needed to swallow her pain medication and anti-nausea pills, but not much more. Obviously, no travel was required. Party central would be Mom's hospital bed brought in for her hospice care weeks earlier. Dad would stay upstairs, in my old childhood bedroom. He was happy to do so. He was four years older than Mom and had lost most of his hearing. We'd have the volume of the TV much too low for him. What's the old adage about two's company?

That evening, about an hour before the debate, I changed into my pajamas and helped Mom get into hers. A sorority sister had given Mom the pajamas after her return from one of her several hospital stays: pink and green — our sorority colors — with Mom's name emblazoned across the back like on an athlete's uniform.

I carefully eased the top over the cute afro she had now that her hair had grown back after her chemo treatment had ended. As I awkwardly threaded her weak arms through the sleeves, I accidentally brushed my knuckles across her nose.

"Oh! You broke my nose! You broke my nose" she cried out.

Mom still had her sense of humor. I'd barely grazed the tip of her nose. I decided to go along with the joke.

"Why did you break my nose?" she continued.

"I'll tell you what," I said. "Since I broke your nose, you can break mine. Then we'll be even."

"I could *never* do that," she said, becoming serious.

"Yes you can," I said.

I took her hand and balled it up into a fist and brushed it against my nose. "My nose is broken now too, and it hurts really bad. Oh, Mommy, I can't believe you broke my nose."

Mom laughed. "You're so silly."

I fluffed her pillow and pressed a button on the bed's remote control so she could sit up comfortably. Then I pulled out my cell phone so we could take selfies. On impulse I said, "Strike a pose, Mommy, like you're a model!"

To my surprise, she obliged, flinging her arms this way and that, raising her chin, tilting her head as I coaxed her along for different poses.

Every so often she'd say. "Is this what you want? Am I doing it right?"

Mom had always been very reserved. She grew up in the 1940s and 50s in a multigenerational household in which children were taught to be seen and not heard. Scolding and punishment didn't come from just her mother, but from anyone else in the house — aunts, uncles, grandparents. Mother said she often retreated to her room and read a book to stay out of the way and avoid anyone's wrath. She mentioned this often as I was growing up, resentment laced in her words. It helped me understand why she often seemed so restrained.

I took one picture after another. I don't know if I could have convinced her to be that spontaneously playful decades earlier. But I believe she knew the importance of the moment and thought about how one day I wouldn't have her anymore.

Mom's world had become small spatially, but I found a way for us to have a big party for two that would have us smiling throughout the evening. And making new memories.

~ 22 ~
Snapshots of a Childhood Summer

Diana Derringer

Lying on our backs watching clouds float by
Running barefoot on narrow creek rock roads
Making forts from discarded sea grass string
Pumping water onto dusty, calloused feet
Taking baths while swimming in ice-cold creeks
Dancing in circles during pop-up showers
Grumbling and sweating, pulling garden weeds
Finding four leaf clover in fields of threes
Munching crisp June apples plucked fresh from trees
Milking cows by hand in shadowy stalls
Letting cats lap foam from warped hubcap bowls
Throwing mealtime scraps to a pack of dogs
Watching tractors chugging down straight crop rows
Picking fencerow blackberries, dodging thorns
Scratching fiery chigger bites all night long
Sewing 4-H crafts for the county fair
Singing to Dad's fiddle come Friday night
Waving funeral-home fans in Sunday school
Joining frog serenades as dark descends
Stepping 'round cousins snoring on the floor
Falling fast asleep in an unspoiled world

~ 23 ~
The Moments I Didn't Pass Up

Tammie Edington Shaw

I sit in my grandfather's favorite rocker in his living room with a box of his treasures on my lap. He recently passed on to his reward after ninety-six years, most of those in ministry.

In the box are daily devotional booklets, gospel tracts, a notebook with lists of names of people who needed prayer. He was a prayer warrior, and he took those needs to God twice a day when he was no longer able to drive and had to be content in his home and backyard. I always thought he'd reinvented himself many times to remain vital.

Now it is Thanksgiving and I am in my hometown for the holiday. Mother wanted me to look through his things and see if there is something I want to keep. I smile as I think about how I am in his rocker just a few feet from the chair where I used to sit. I'm so glad I made the four-hour trip as often as I could to sit in that chair and talk with him . . . or rather, communicate with our made-up sign language and written notes because his hearing was almost nonexistent.

I'm so glad I sat at the kitchen table in the adjoining room to have breakfast with him. I would rise before daylight and walk over to his house, next door to my mother's home. When I opened the back door I could hear him praying aloud to God. I often stood and listened for a while to the holy conversation between him and the Lord. Then I went to the living room door and waved to let him know I was there before going to the kitchen to make breakfast. We'd sit together at the table and he would point to me to pray for the meal. I prayed as loud as I could and then squeezed his hand, to let him know I'd finished the prayer. He talked to me about how breakfast was his favorite meal and what a good job I had done preparing it. He would reminisce about his life and how happy he was that he had made some of the choices he did to pray at this person's bedside or visit another person at the nursing home. I listened and acknowledged him with a nod of my head.

While I cleaned the kitchen he would return to the living room and read the newspaper I had brought in. In the afternoon after he had taken a nap, I would come back and escort him to the swing in his back yard. I joined him there as we swayed slowly back and forth while he told me how he had come to know Christ. Tears ran down his face, because it was just as real to him then as it had been all those years earlier.

I now find tears running down my cheeks as I sit in his chair and remember. I rejoice that I made those decisions to be with him. I wouldn't trade those times for anything. I have no moments to regret, only moments to treasure.

~ 24 ~
The Philly Ice Cream Parlor

Lola Di Giulio De Maci

When I was seven years old, my mom and I traveled by train from Canton, Ohio, to Philadelphia, Pennsylvania. Until then the only train I had been familiar with was the American Flyer that ran in circles under the Christmas tree every year. If you pressed a small white button on a piece of plywood, the train's whistle shrieked loud and clear, letting you know that it would be flying around the bend. I loved that train and its whistly wail. It was a wonderful part of my childhood.

This trip would not only be my first experience on a train, but also the very first time I would meet my Godparents, Sam and Ernestine. "We'll go to Philadelphia for a vacation," Mom said. "We'll have fun."

But there was another reason for the trip. When I was five years old, I had undergone a splenectomy; at six years, a tonsillectomy. Now, at seven, I was a skinny little thing in need of some tender-loving care and "fattening up."

Philadelphia, the City of Brotherly Love. Good choice.

We packed our bags and headed east.

My journey to wellness had begun.

The first thing I noticed when Mom and I approached my

godparents' house was how very long it was. It seemed to go on forever. But during the time we spent there, I came to realize that it was part of what they called "row houses," houses attached to each other with no yard in-between. Kind of like box cars of a train attached to each other, following one another in a row. I could even see all the backyards of the people who lived in the row houses on this block because the yards were separated by chain-link fences. I was enchanted.

While Godmother Ernestine and Mom would make supper, I would play in the backyard with my only friend, my little rubber ball that had a face painted on it.

I spent hours bouncing my ball up and down, up and down on a cement sidewalk, waiting impatiently for my godfather to come home from work — because, every day after dinner, I would grab his hand and the two of us would dash across the street to the ice cream parlor where I could choose any flavor I wanted.

"Vanilla, please," I would invariably say, my smile a mile wide. Then, "See you tomorrow!"

With my creamy treat in one hand and Sam's hand in the other, my heart skipped with joy as we left the forty other creamy flavors behind.

The routine never varied, until one late afternoon in the fall when Sam said he needed to do something before we went for ice cream. The weather outside was getting nippy, so he had to prepare the furnace for winter.

We headed down the wooden steps to the basement, and Sam opened the coal chute. A steel container at the bottom of the chute aroused my curiosity.

"What's this, Sam?"

"Well, it's going to be a surprise. You'll see."

My eyes grew wide as suddenly, big, shiny black pieces of coal — coal that would provide fuel for the furnace and keep our house warm for the season — came rushing down the chute from somewhere outside, resulting in a loud *bang* when they landed in the steel container.

Of course, after the coal was all loaded, off to the ice cream parlor we went.

Sam and Ernestine are gone now, but I will never forget them. They have seeded themselves somewhere down deep in my soul, touching that place in my heart reserved as "For Godparents Only." I think back fondly on those kind, beautiful people who took me and my mom into their home because this skinny little girl needed healing.

I'm now a mother of three, a retired schoolteacher, and someone who is grateful for all her blessings.

~ 25 ~

Twice Owned

Janet Faye Mueller

"Do you recognize this?" my sister asked me in a note accompanied by a photo of a blue blouse. I thought to myself, "No, should I?"

After pondering the photo for a while, I remembered she used to wear a blouse like it back in the 70's. But why was she sending me a picture of it?

When I called her to ask for an explanation, she told me an incredible story.

She had stopped at a Des Moines area vintage clothing store she had never been in before. Her gaze landed upon a blouse, and she felt very drawn to it. Studying it carefully, she noted that the blouse was handmade with a hand-embroidered piece in the center. The seams had flaws, and the zipper was not sewn in straight.

Then, it dawned on her. She had made this very blouse herself! She'd worn it when she was in high school forty years ago ... in our hometown about one hundred miles from Des Moines.

How in the world did it get into this used clothing store?

She concluded that she had probably given boxes of clothing to Goodwill when she moved into her current house over thirty years ago. Someone had evidently bought the blouse and recently decided to sell it in the consignment shop my sister just happened to walk into that particular day.

She bought the blouse, of course, expensive as it was! It was her blouse, after all, now twice owned — once by virtue of creation, and once by virtue of paying the price.

Have you ever lost or sold something you made only to have it returned many years later? Do you know the feeling of joyous astonishment? These kinds of stories tug at our hearts because they speak a universal truth to us. That which someone creates will always hold a piece of their heart. Even if it is lost or sold, in an abstract sense, it remains theirs because they created it. They hold a type of ownership over it because it originated in their mind or imagination.

So it is with our Creator. He made us, and He wants us back. He loves and likes us despite our flaws. We will always hold a piece of His heart.

~ 26 ~
Derby Day

Annmarie B. Tait

As jockeys mount their horses to the whispering strains of "My Old Kentucky Home," a gentle breeze ripples through the sea of wide-brimmed hats that adorn the southern belles perched in the grandstand. The annual Run for the Roses, The Kentucky Derby, captures the heart of every true Kentuckian — and a few others as well.

As for Daddy, he played the horses all his life although he never placed a bet. Taking care of a family of seven, including my stay-at-home Mom, blew a sizable hole through his paycheck. Excess cash for gambling was a luxury he never enjoyed. Instead, he tracked his imaginary wins and losses in a small spiral notebook tucked in the side cushion of his favorite chair.

Luckily, Daddy never let a minor detail like lack of funds stop us from celebrating the Run for the Roses at our house. Perhaps not as elegantly, but certainly with as much enthusiasm as Churchill Downs ever saw.

Each year just before the race, Daddy jotted down the names of the top seven favorites on separate slips of paper and dropped them into an old fish bowl. He placed the fish bowl in the center of the kitchen table where we gathered, eager to place our twenty-five cent bets.

When we were all seated Daddy bellowed, always in a most official tone, "Place Your Bets." One by one our quarters clanked to the bottom of an old china teacup as we passed it around, followed by the glass fish bowl from which we each drew the name of our "lucky" horse.

As we did this, Mom put together our traditional Derby Day fare of lemonade with a sprig of mint for our faux mint juleps, cheeseburgers, potato salad, pickles, and homemade rice pudding. We gobbled it down in the living room, a rare treat indeed, as we sat on the floor with our eyes glued to our TV set.

It was quite a gala.

Though an allowance was unheard of, I did earn ten cents every Saturday by shining Daddy's shoes — a daunting task indeed considering his eighteen-year history with the U.S. Marine Corps. On many a Saturday he returned his shoes for me to buff and rebuff until they passed inspection. So for me, quarters were hard to come by, and even harder to part with. But the idea of winning a whole dollar and seventy-five cents drew me in every time.

My most memorable Derby happened in 1970. That year I had my eye on a stylish orange juice pitcher and six matching glasses, displayed in the window of The Bright Spot, our local five-and-dime store. The dainty pitcher and footed glasses gleamed with brilliant oranges and bright green leaves. I had my heart set on giving Mom this most elegant glassware for Mother's Day, but it would be impossible without winning the Kentucky Derby purse, because the price was three dollars and fifty cents. Even though I had already saved two dollars and fifty cents, I still needed nearly the entire pot to pay the balance and buy wrapping paper.

I sat at the table, hands resting in my lap, my fingers crossed. When my turn arrived, I dropped my quarter in the cup and my sister slid the fish bowl in front of me. Slowly I pulled out one of the last two slips of paper and unfolded it to reveal the name of my horse: My Dad George. No one paid any attention to the remaining folded slip of paper at the bottom of the bowl. That was my brother's horse. Daddy insisted on throwing a quarter in the pot for him even though he had moved away from home a few months earlier.

As the horses took off down the track I sat on the floor watching intently and drew even closer to the TV screen trying to send a telepathic message to My Dad George.

By the time they rounded the final turn, My Dad George started moving forward and I began to perk up. My Dad George gave one terrific effort but finished in second place. My hopes fell to the floor with a thud.

As the winning horse, Dust Commander, sailed across the finish line silence fell in our living room. In unison our heads turned toward the kitchen table where the fish bowl sat holding that last folded piece of paper. Then my older sister tore a path to the kitchen and grabbed it.

Wouldn't you just know it? Dust Commander lurked at the bottom of the bowl. The winning horse defaulted to my brother who wasn't even there for the race.

I shook my head in disbelief, certain there was no such thing as justice in this world. Then I shuffled up to my room and sulked over not being able to buy the pitcher and glasses.

Later that evening my brother called.

"Your horse won," I said. "Dust Commander won the Kentucky Derby."

He thought for a moment and then said, "Well, that's not right. I wasn't even there. Tell Daddy to give the money to the second place winner."

"Are you kidding?" I blurted out.

"The horse that came in second was My Dad George, and that was my horse!"

"Well," he said, "don't spend it all in one place."

But spend it all in one place I did, with enough money left over to have the sales lady wrap it professionally. The top of the box sported a bow made of sparkly clear straws drawn tight in the center then fanning out. This was one dramatic bow. Mom said it was almost too pretty to unwrap so she saved it for last.

Once opened, Mom beamed. She immediately placed the set on display in the china cabinet and we used them only on birthdays and holidays . . . proving, at least to me, how very valuable they were to her.

It had been years since I'd thought about the Kentucky Derby when I caught a glimpse of a TV screen as I passed through Macy's. A small crowd gathered around, but I think I was more excited than most.

When the horses headed for the starting gate, I reached into my pocket and pulled out a shiny quarter. In the back of my mind the distant echo of Daddy's booming voice urged me to place my bet.

I traveled back in time to the days when Daddy's enthusiasm for simple pleasures silently shaped the person I am today. It is not a trip I take often, but when I do I linger in the presence of his awesome character, his kind heart, and his fun-loving soul.

As the crowd at Macy's cheered, I snapped back to reality and walked away. I didn't hang around to find out who won. My priceless childhood memories make me the wealthiest Kentucky Derby winner of all time. Daddy saw to that. And he did it with nothing more than a little imagination and an old fish bowl.

~ 27 ~
The Sparrow May Fall

Carol Graham

He was sitting there, so very tiny, right in the middle of the intersection. But as I looked closely, I saw him quivering. I was appalled and astonished when no one stopped long enough for him to fly away. No one seemed to care. Cars from both directions drove right over him and each one barely missed hitting him. I had nearly driven over him myself and knew it was inevitable that he would die.

My thoughts immediately went to the Bible, which tells us that God sees the sparrow fall. I watched that sparrow and knew I had to take action.

As I watched that bird on the road, adrenalin soared through me. I got out of my car in the middle of the intersection and raised my hands to stop all traffic from each direction. My steps seemed to be in slow motion as I was met with horns honking and people shouting obscenities, but my focus was not on them. My focus was on the sparrow. I knew what I had to do. I had to save that little bird, and nothing else mattered.

I knew that if God sees that sparrow fall, He also sees me when I struggle and fall. These are the times when we need to be reminded of how much God loves us. The Bible tells us that He knows us intimately; even the hairs on our heads are numbered — no matter how many we may lose in any given day.

In the book of Psalms, David tells us that God has named every single star in the heavens — all forty septillion. To help understand how many that is, there are only approximately five hundred thousand words in the American dictionary. It would take eighty quadrillion books of that size to list the stars' names.

If God knows the names of each of the stars, *He knows your name.* He knew you before you were born. His love for you is beyond anything you could begin to comprehend.

Each step I took closer to that little bird intensified my determination to save it. I bent down and gently picked him up and carried him to safety under a shrub on the corner. As I headed back to my car, instead of honking and cursing, I heard applause for my good deed. I felt exhilarated.

Then the strangest thing happened. I had a strong sense that God was speaking to my heart. "How do you feel?"

"What do you mean how do I feel?" I thought. "Isn't it obvious? I feel wonderful." I wanted to add, "What a ridiculous question; God should know how I feel." But He was asking me so I would take notice. He was about to teach me something about His love for me.

I had a warm sense He was smiling at me, "Now you have an idea of how I feel when you fall down and I pick you up and take you to safety."

I was amazed. I had always beaten myself up for the stupid mistakes I had made in my life and now it was as if God was saying how much He enjoyed being there to help me, to protect me and to shield me. To pick me up.

It made me realize the need to share stories, simple stories, to explain God's love. Even though I have been a Christian all my life, I am constantly reminded of that little sparrow. I share this story in a variety of ways with people who have a hard time relating to such an intimate relationship with our heavenly Father.

He wants us to know how much He loves us.

Every. Single. Day.

As we become more aware of God's great love for us, we need to celebrate what it means to us by sharing His love with friends and family. In the world's current climate, they need the message of love more than ever before.

God truly loves each one of us. Of that, I have no doubt. First John 4:10 (KJV) states it this way: *Herein is love, not that we loved God, but that He loved us, and sent His Son to be the propitiation for our sins.*

~ 28 ~

The Playhouse

Beverly Hill McKinney

The playhouse. What memories!

I was born the youngest of four children in the early 40s in Pacific Grove, California. My sister was two years older than me and my two brothers were six and eight years older. Because of the age difference of my brothers, my sister and I were closer and spent long hours together.

We shared lots of those hours in our playhouse.

I was very young when Dad built our playhouse. He found a large wooden packing crate, which he decided would be perfect. He set the crate on a cement foundation, roofed it with shingles, and made two windows and a door in the front. Then he covered the floor with linoleum and reinforced the walls with heavy cardboard.

Our playhouse was a source of many hours of fun and laughter for us. As a very young child I would take my dolls out to the playhouse and have tea parties. My sister, Zoe, more of a tomboy, would take her little model cars and play with them while I was enjoying my tea parties.

As time went on and we grew older, we decided that we would be marine biologists and learn about sea life in our playhouse. Because we lived within walking distance of the Pacific Ocean, we would gather up specimens and take them home to look at and experiment with. I well remember one instance when we had seen some dried sea stars in a local novelty store and decided that we could do that ourselves. We found a sea star washed up on the beach and took it home to dry. However, since both of us had lots of homework that week we had no time to spend in our playhouse. At the end of the week, as my mother was hanging clothes on the clothesline she smelled a horrid odor.

Was that coming from the playhouse? she wondered.

She asked us what we were doing in the playhouse.

Zoe looked at me and said, "Bev, you did put that starfish out in the sun, didn't you?"

Shamefully I looked down and said, "Sorry, I forgot."

We soon learned what the odor was. It took nearly a week for the smell of a rotten starfish to clear out enough that we could once again play inside.

After this incident we decided to grow frogs. In the wintertime, water formed small pools in a pine forest very near our house. These held scores of tadpoles. Grabbing quart canning jars from Mom we would race up to the "ponds" and gather tadpoles to bring home. Dad had made us two aquariums and we used these to grow our frogs. We watched in fascination as our tadpoles slowly turned into tiny frogs. After they became frogs, we put them out in our parent's large vegetable garden. I don't know if they survived, but both Mom and Dad would compliment us on keeping the bugs down in the garden.

For our next project we decided we would have a church service for the neighbor kids and their pets. We made printed bulletins using crayons. My sister's small recorder supplied our music. We arranged little chairs in aisles. Free candy for each participant brought out our friends. I think the one who listened the best was our family dog, Blackie.

When we were nearing high school age, we decided to turn the playhouse into our personal place to study and relax. We took out a couple of old easy chairs and had Dad hook up a light bulb. We also hooked up a radio so we could listen to music. How many happy hours we spent doing homework and just hanging out together as sisters!

After we left home, Dad, who was a retired telegrapher, decided to make the playhouse his radio shack. He built himself a desk on which he put his beloved Underwood typewriter and hooked up his short wave and his telegraph key. Dad spent many hours in his retirement years exchanging messages in Morse code with friends around the world. He put a large map of the world on the wall and as he made new contacts he would put a pushpin in those areas.

When both our parents passed away, we had to make the decision to sell the house. It was very hard to leave the home that Dad and Mom had lived in for over fifty years. However, the hardest part was leaving our playhouse and the memories made there. After the sale of the house, I was visiting the area while on vacation. As I drove past our old home, I decided to stop and see the remodeling that was in progress. After asking permission, I looked over the back fence. To my horror I realized our playhouse had been torn down. How sad I was to think that other kids would not be able to have the adventures we had in our beloved playhouse.

~ 29 ~

Crochet

Amari Seymour

Do you remember
The day you taught me
To crochet, Mom?
The last light of morning
Streamed through the window.
You and I sat together.
You crocheting. Me learning.
"First thing you want to do,"
You said, "is make a chain."
I made an inquiry of the meaning.
"A chain is the desired length
Of what your project is," was your reply.
"What are you making?"
"A blanket for your niece," you said.
"Now hush and listen.
"Yarn over, hook, pull through.
"Yarn over, hook, pull through.
"Now you try," you said
Handing me the hook and yarn.
"Like this?" I asked
Copying the movements
You told me.
"Yes," was your reply.
Do you remember that day?
Do you remember teaching me to crochet?

~ 30 ~
Working for My Good

Norma C. Mezoe

As soon as I placed my foot on the edge of the porch, I knew I was in trouble. I remember thinking, "Oh, no! I'm going to fall!" As I toppled through the air over the steps, I tried to catch myself, but it was impossible. I hit the sidewalk face first, with a hard thud.

I was at my older neighbor's house. For many years, there had been a ramp leading off the porch because my neighbor walked with a walker. She had gone to live in a nursing home a short time before this, and the ramp had been removed. I remembered too late.

In the emergency room, I was diagnosed with a hematoma, bleeding on the brain, a concussion, and small seizures. The doctors sent me by ambulance to a hospital specializing in brain injuries. For two days I hovered near death as my family hovered near me. After being in the hospital for eight days, I was transferred to a rehab facility closer to home.

This was a new experience for me. I had visited patients in nursing homes many times, but now I was the one being visited. I learned what it was like to need to go to the bathroom, but to have to wait until an employee was available to take me because

I was forbidden to go anywhere by myself.

With my bruised and swollen face, I looked as though I had been in a fight and lost every round. Eventually my appearance returned to normal. Simple therapy began immediately, and I pushed myself to do whatever the therapists suggested.

Even though my recovery was proceeding well, although slowly, other problems crept in and one day, they threatened to overwhelm me. The dark, emotional clouds gathered over my head and threatened to drown me in self-pity.

I knew I could lie in bed and let the "poor me's" blanket me in defeat, or I could stop feeling sorry for myself. I could reach out to others in the nursing home whose problems were more serious than mine.

Day by day I pushed myself to eat the healthy food served — food I didn't eat at home. I realized it would increase my lagging strength. Hour after hour, with my therapist's help, I walked with a walker, rode a stationary bike and did various exercises.

The first time I tried to walk without a walker was a frightening experience. Even though the therapist was holding tightly to the support belt around my waist, I still felt as though I was falling, and I cried out in alarm.

At times I wondered if I would ever walk without assistance.

Through the encouragement of the therapists and my family, I persisted. I was aware many people were praying for my healing and that helped give me the determination to continue my efforts.

I discovered a small waiting room that was always empty, and I began wheeling myself there in the early evenings. I could look out the window at the countryside's autumn scenery. Sometimes I sang hymns softly.

I looked forward to those times of refreshment.

Finally, came the time I had really looked forward to — Going home day! I had been in the rehab for thirty-three days. I had experienced days of challenge such as coping with wavering emotions, living with a roommate, and the daily routine of therapy, but with the Lord's help, I not only endured, I met my goal.

One of my favorite Bible verses is Romans 8:28 KJV: *We know that all things work together for good to them that love God, to them who are the called according to his purpose.*

Many years earlier I had begun claiming that verse as a promise of God's faithfulness when I was going through another trial.

My husband left our home late one night. I waited through long and lonely hours for his return. During that time, I learned he had been having an affair with a young wife and mother. They had driven off at midnight together.

When he returned the next morning, it was only to gather his clothing and belongings. Eventually, he filed for divorce, and I began my life as a single person.

Later, in an article published in a national Christian magazine, I wrote about his leaving, and the many ways in which God had worked and was working in my life at that time. One of those was opening the door to a job so I could support myself.

As a result of the article, I received many letters and phone calls from people scattered across the United States. God worked good from bad (Romans 8:28) by using the article to encourage others who were struggling with heartbreaking circumstances.

What good has God brought through the pain, frustration, and the state of being dependent upon others to meet my needs that I experienced in the rehab? After being a patient myself, I have more compassion and understanding of the frustrations and helplessness patients experience. Now I can emphathize with their needs.

Perhaps you have gone through similar problems. Or, your heartaches and challenges may be completely different from mine. Be assured that the Lord walks with you through your valley and He will use every despairing moment to draw you nearer to Him and to work for your good.

When we surrender our lives to the Lord, He can use all of our circumstances to bring about good in our lives. And not only in our lives, but also in the lives of others.

God does work for good in all things in the lives of Christians. He is the giver of treasured moments.

~ 312 ~

War Dogs

Robert B. Robeson

This story with its human, plus dog participants and combat events happened nearly fifty-five years ago in Southeast Asia during the Vietnam War. All that's left of this interaction — after many of the enlisted men and officers/aviators have passed on to their eternal rewards — are the reoccurring thoughts of those remaining who remember the unique combat relationship and close companionship we experienced with our menagerie of dogs in a war zone.

The 236th Medical Detachment (Helicopter Ambulance) was located at Red Beach on the picturesque shore of Da Nang Harbor in Da Nang, South Vietnam in 1969-1970. Our fifty-man unit was authorized six UH1H (Huey) helicopters. We used them to evacuate wounded soldiers and civilians, from both sides of the action, to battalion aid stations located at Landing Zones Baldy and Hawk Hill, and to hospital ships and a variety of military and civilian hospitals in Da Nang.

We soon learned that war was emotionally, psychologically, physically, and spiritually disturbing. It was a world of creative cruelty. Life in this unbelievable realm was bloody. It was messy. It could be scary. In my own case as a U.S. Army captain and evacuation pilot, assigned as detachment operations officer and later commander, it meant striving to keep as many people alive in our operational area as possible.

When I first arrived at Red Beach, there were only two dogs in our detachment: Big Dusty and Jackie. Big Dusty was a large alpha male and Jackie, his sister, was a smaller white female. It wasn't long after my arrival that a variety of other dogs began to mysteriously appear in enlisted and officer hootches. It was obvious clandestine contacts had been forged in the local community. Money talked and allowed these animals to enter into a different community of foreigners.

This was something that has occurred with American soldiers in every war our country has ever fought. It wasn't long before most of us realized that these four-legged fur balls were having a positive effect on unit personnel.

One reason was that our enlisted soldiers, whose average age during this conflict was nineteen, were often apprehensive and afraid a long way from home. These dogs helped fill a void reminiscent of other pets they'd been surrounded with growing up. When they took responsibility for an animal's needs, it helped take their minds off what they were forced to experience and witness in aerial combat nearly every day. It was also apparent that they relished the unconditional love these canines brought to their war world.

A dog's innate nature to please, and their constant presence, reminded us that we weren't alone. We interacted with them as though we were twelve-year-olds again. In a traumatic and ugly world that seemed remote and unreal most of the time, they helped quiet the confusing voices and persistent noise in our heads. Even grown men without an animal companion can seem like a body without a soul. Nothing can be as beneficial for soldier morale as adequate sleep, good food, letters from home, and being surrounded by a pack of playful dogs.

Most of the time flight crews would return from dangerous and demanding missions looking and smelling like refugees from *The Grapes of Wrath* novel. Yet we could always count on the canine contingent being there to greet us, their tails wagging like windshield wipers, when our three-quarter-ton truck ferried pilots, medics, and crew chiefs back to operations from our flight line next to the beach. When we dismounted, they'd vie with each other for position and surround us as though we were rock stars. They always managed to wring smiles from even the weariest and most frazzled of crewmembers. And whether it was the middle of the day or night, they weren't impressed by anyone's rank when they nuzzled a hand or exposed arm with a wet nose or tongue to welcome us back.

Toward the end of 1969, one of our commissioned pilots was given a gray female puppy by his girlfriend. She was a nurse at the 95th Evacuation Hospital — located across town on China Beach next to the South China Sea — who later became his wife. He named the pup Little Dusty. She was a real sweetheart and the friendliest of all our dogs.

Another puppy that showed up belonged to a warrant officer pilot whose alternate call sign was "The Mexican." He named her *Pachuca,* which had a Spanish connotation that has escaped my memory after all of these decades. Pachuca was a dark-brown bundle of energy that loved to chase her tail and perform a crazy little dance whenever anyone attempted to pet or pick her up. She was a squirmy bundle of continuous motion.

Both Little Dusty and Pachuca were as perky as rats in liverwurst. And speaking of rats, this is where our dogs would unite in battling a common foe. Vietnamese rats that resided in hootch ceilings or under buildings in our compound were not of the Lillliputian variety. Many of them were as large as small cats. Big Dusty — the local enforcer — was a rat's worst nightmare. For a rat to expose itself on the ground in our unit area, with him around, was as smart as shaving your beard with a lawnmower.

When Big Dusty cornered one of these sneaky and annoying critters, the other dogs would block all escape routes and begin barking and growling until he dispatched the intruder on his home turf. Some rats were so big they'd turn and try to fight him but that was always a bad decision. After he'd made the kill, he'd often carry the deceased around in his mouth until he chose someone to give it to. He'd drop the still-warm corpse at this person's feet as though he were bestowing a gift. Perhaps he was merely making a dog point by attempting to prove that he was actually earning his keep.

These canine companions circulated among unit members, both officer and enlisted personnel, whomever needed an emotional lift at the moment. None of them slept outside. They were either formally invited to spend the night in a hootch or would use their own initiative to procure appropriate quarters. They were family and we all looked out for each other.

These funny, fiesty and friendly dogs helped us cope with

life's combat burdens, boredom, and often, brevity. They were our personal cadre of psychologists, psychiatrists, and therapists who didn't mind living with us on our compound in what most Americans would describe as a third-world ghetto existence.

Being surrounded by these animals, with their unconditional love, lightened our human cares and fears, and drew all of us closer together. They gave us the extraordinary gift of themselves during our tumultuous time in 'Nam. They were a special part of our lives then and still remain so to this day, over half a century later.

It's possible that their paw prints will remain forever imprinted on a diminishing group of old combat veterans' hearts for as long as they continue to beat. These dogs are still mentioned with regularity and warmth in letters between remaining unit members and at our unit reunions. How could it be otherwise?

~ 32 ~

In Memory of Dazzle

Lola Di Giulio De Maci

"The fish is dead!" Those were the first four words I heard when I entered my second grade classroom one morning.

Oh, great! I thought. *A dead fish.* Right then I knew it was going to be a long day. I had one-hundred-and-one things on my to-do list. I didn't need a dead fish.

Sam, who loved researching anything on Attila the Hun, stood at attention with a net ready to scoop the departed fish out of the tank.

"Shall I flush him down the toilet?" he asked. "Or throw him in the trash can?"

I couldn't think fast enough. What does one do with a fish that's left the pond? Because death might be a new experience for some of the students — and since I didn't want the toilet/trash can thing — I suggested we bury him. After all, Dazzle deserved a proper burial for being a classroom-friendly goldfish.

My mind raced. What should Dazzle be placed in for burial? Where do we bury him? What do we dig the grave with? What kind of a service should we hold? Will I get in trouble if I bring up the "God of Dead Fish" in a eulogy?

The kids were in mourning, and I needed grown-up support

and direction. So I decided to call the school office. I was careful how to phrase my questions because twenty grief-stricken second graders were at my side, listening to every word I was saying.

"We have a dead fish in our room," I heard myself say. "His name is Dazzle, and we want to bury him." I told the staff what had just happened and that I wanted to do right by the kids and Dazzle. I then asked about any procedures I should follow in meeting the school's rules. That is, if they had any for this kind of occasion.

Giggling turned to laughter on the other end of the line.

"Hey, you guys, this isn't funny," I whispered into the mouthpiece. "We're in mourning here."

After the giggles subsided in the office, we received instructions as to what we were permitted to do with the body. With that, the class and I headed outdoors to the soft dirt that would be Dazzle's final resting place.

Having picked out a burial plot, we proceeded to place Dazzle in a napkin and dig the grave with a white plastic spoon. We then decided to honor him with a song.

"What shall we sing?" I asked twenty solemn apprentices. One of the kids started singing "God Bless America."

"Oh, no!" I interrupted abruptly . . . and then realized I should have let him sing it through. But we were running out of time. "We don't need a flag song," I said apologetically. "We need a fish song."

The class didn't know a fish song. So Crystal — the classroom soloist and future Diana Ross — composed one on the spot. We all listened intently.

"The fish is d-e-e-e-a-d!" she sang, swaying to and fro, her face pointing heavenward. "The fish is d-e-e-e-a-d!"

I followed her song with the eulogy.

"I really didn't know you well, Dazzle," I began, "but I'm sure you were a good fish. Everyone in the class thought you were a good fish, too. We'll miss you."

Just then I heard a little voice to my right say, "I know who killed you, Dazzle. It was Bubbles."

Bubbles was Dazzle's tank mate. It was hard to keep my composure. I didn't want to be like the gigglers at the other end of the phone earlier that morning.

When the service was over, it was time for recess. I welcomed a change of pace and a chance to look over the day's lesson plans. But ear-piercing wailing suddenly interrupted my thoughts.

"Dazzle is gone! Someone stole Dazzle!"

Someone had gone to the soft dirt where Dazzle lay and had dug him up. The kids were traumatized and immediately went into mourning all over again.

"Now what?" I thought.

We all gathered in a group on the classroom rug, sitting in a circle, holding hands. We talked openly about our beloved pet and what he had meant to each one of us. When all was said and done, the class decided that Bubbles was innocent and that he would be the new class mascot.

It was also decided that someone would have to feed Bubbles, clean his tank, and take care of him. Sam volunteered for the job. But first . . . he would make sure there was enough time in his day to research Attila the Hun.

~ 33 ~
Mom's Never-Failing Gift

Diana Derringer

I had settled into my dorm room, survived the first few weeks of life away from home, and established a routine for classes and study. With a mixture of excitement and uncertainty, I looked forward to campus life.

My parents had instilled the habit of daily devotional time, so I opened my Bible for a few moments alone with God. As I turned the pages, a previously unnoticed scrap of paper caught my attention. A one-by-two-inch, 16-line poem lay before me. Although signed *Mom*, I would have known the source without her signature. The lower right edge pointed toward the first Bible verse my mother taught me: *"Do not be overcome by evil, but overcome evil with good"* (Romans 12:21 NIV).

I've never known anyone else to claim Romans 12:21 as their first memory verse. I don't recall the details of learning it. However, in my home church, children and adults often quoted memorized Bible verses as a part of Sunday morning opening exercises. I'm sure I practiced as Mom listened during the week before I shared it. Both the words and the message of that verse have challenged and guided me through the years. Mom never had eyes in the back of her head. Far better, she gave the never-failing gift of scripture in my heart.

Never-Failing Truth for Youth

When I faced temptation, both as a child and a teen, Romans 12:21 often came to mind. If someone hurt me, and I wanted to get even, Romans 12:21 told me not to do it. It offered clear guidance and kept me out of a world of trouble. That's not to say my desire for revenge never drowned out the verse's truth. However, when that happened, the after-effects of following my stubborn pride made me one miserable youngster.

When I was encouraged to join in questionable activities, Romans 12:21 returned. Again, I didn't always listen, but I'm thankful for the times I did. If I went along with a misguided crowd, I learned that such activity created a void in my life. It separated me from what I knew was right, leaving me guilt-ridden and ready to return to God's goodness.

I remember one night in high school, during an out-of-state teen convention, I ate dinner with a group of new friends. When I mentioned the approaching curfew, one girl assured us her parent was a leader, so curfew was no problem. However, when we returned a few minutes late, our chaperones expressed their concern in no uncertain terms. Romans 12:21 led me to apologize the following morning and assure the adults in charge I would not be late again.

Never-Failing Truth for Adults

In some ways, the temptations of adulthood differ from those of earlier years, but those differences make them no less appealing. Fudging on time sheets, taking shortcuts on assignments, giving less than my best at work — everyone else does it, so why not? Romans 12:21, that's why.

Turn a blind eye to obvious indiscretions, ignore inconvenient laws, fail to file honest reports — I can't do those either, according to Romans 12:21.

Smear the name of those who smear mine, show disrespect to those who fail to respect me, mistreat those who mistreat me. Nope. Romans 12:21 says otherwise.

Timeless Truth

Regardless of my age, Romans 12:21 holds true. Giving evil for evil, following a wayward crowd, and yielding to temptation always make matters worse.

Only good triumphs over evil. Yet, I can't become good enough on my own. That's why Jesus came. He died on the cross for my evil, and He covered it with His righteousness, His goodness, when I accepted Him as Savior and Lord.

That's the message Mom taught. Her never-failing gift, for which I'm eternally grateful.

~ 34 ~
Singing Songs of Love

Terri Elders

In 1955 "Love Is a Many Splendored Thing," featuring The Four Aces' close harmonies, spilled out from every Southern California jukebox and car radio. When Bob Elders and I caught the movie by the same name at our local drive in, we knew we wanted its theme song for our upcoming wedding.

Who could resist the lyrics?

Once on a high and windy hill, In the morning mist
Two lovers kissed, and the world stood still

When we sat down at a local Lutheran church to plan our June nuptials, the whitehaired pastor unceremoniously nixed it.

"No. Absolutely not," he'd said, with a starchy scowl. "How about 'A Mighty Fortress Is Our God?'"

We negotiated. His suggestions, so solemn, so heavily churchy, did not enchant us. Finally, we agreed to compromise on an Irving Berlin classic, "Always."

When I informed my sister, who'd be soloist, of the choice, she snickered. "Waltzy schmaltzy."

"Well, Berlin wrote it for a wedding," my fiancé explained. "A wedding gift to his own bride in 1926." Bob, several years my senior, always leaned a little Old School.

"Always," lacking the fervor of our first choice, nonetheless conveyed a heartwarming message. Even so, as my sister crooned I envisioned those lovers on their hill.

A few years ago, as our son, Steve, and his fiancé, Helayne, planned their summer wedding, I speculated about what music they'd choose. Steve, widowed several years earlier, had found love again, overwhelming me with joy. Helayne, for decades a pal of both Steve and his late wife, had been single for a long while.

I figured the music would be heavy with sixties hits. When I told friends, "I bet the wedding music is going to be all Beatles songs," we reminisced about music we'd loved back in the day.

"But I can't be certain," I added. "The bride might have some songs in mind, as well."

Steve had confided he'd given the DJ the playlist, but he didn't share it with me. Since Steve's childhood friend, a professional actor, would officiate at this wedding at a venue other than a church, I knew there'd be no censorship of choices.

Recalling my conservative ceremony, I felt a bit envious.

In 1964, when "I Want to Hold Your Hand" hit American pop charts, Steve was six years old. Because Bob worked nights, Steve and I had evenings to ourselves. While I corrected homework papers, we'd listen on our portable radio to legendary sportscaster Vin Scully call the play-by-play for our beloved Dodgers.

When the British Invasion hit the airways, we'd tune in to a Top 30 station during supper. Since Steve spent most of his allowance on Beatles fan clubs, fanzines filled our mailbox. Steve would read me the latest gossip about the Fab Four's sweethearts, or how the clubs sponsored children in Kenya and the Philippines for school tuition and books.

"Listen to what George Harrison's sister says!" he'd exclaim. I'd smile and nod.

By 1968, Steve hunkered down at the kitchen counter every Wednesday night as KHJ's Sam Riddle counted down the Boss 30. Steve meticulously recorded the hits in his blue notebook. He'd already been collecting 45 rpms for well over a year.

"I hear music in my head," Steve once confided. I asked if he wanted to take piano or guitar lessons. "No, I just love to listen."

Over the years his collection burgeoned. He turned from singles to LPs, and later to 8-tracks, cassettes, and finally to CDs. In recent decades he's shared obscure cuts with Southland Golden Oldies radio stations.

The wedding venue, a rustic saloon called the Orange County Mining Company, offered a stunning panoramic sunset view of the lights of the southland valley.

When Steve and Helayne read their vows, I wasn't surprised when my son promised his bride that he'd follow the advice delivered by four wise men a half century earlier. "I'll love you 'Eight Days a Week,'" he pledged.

Then Steve, like his dad before him, leaned Old School. No, he didn't quote from "Always." He said he'd been captivated by "The Way You Look Tonight," from the first time he'd heard it. Its lyrics painted a picture nearly as romantic as those lovers kissing on that high and windy hill. He gazed at Helayne and read:

> "Someday, when I'm awfully low
> When the world is cold
> I will feel a glow just thinking of you,
> And the way you look tonight."

Then the DJ played "Eight Days a Week," and guests all boogied down the satin carpet, rocking to the irresistible Beatles rhythm. The newlyweds' inaugural dance to Linda Ronstadt's version of Randy Newman's "Feels Like Home," couldn't have been a more tender selection.

I later learned that this was Helayne's choice.

When the couple had invited me, as the final surviving parent, the chance to offer the first toast, I knew exactly how I'd begin . . . with a Beatles song, of course.

Toasting the newlyweds, I alluded to "Your Mother Should Know," and what this mother did know. I confirmed that Steve's dad, who'd died a decade earlier, would be grinning in Heaven.

At least one of the songs the DJ played turned out to be a hit before this mother was born. "The Way You Look Tonight" by Jerome Kern and Dorothy Field, from the 1936 Fred Astaire film "Swing Time," won the Academy Award for Best Song.

The newlyweds recently celebrated their fifth anniversary. Both have retired from their longtime jobs and now travel extensively.

This mother would guess that they often find moments to embrace on high and windy hills.

~ 35 ~
About Winter

Sue Rice

My favorite things about the winter season are the ones
   that only God knows how to make.
Take for instance, the diamonds in the snow,
   shining even in the dark of night.
They cover the ground and reflect the sun
   and the moon's glow.
I love it when the snow falls, and the trees look as though
   they have white frosting on all their branches.
How is it that each snowflake is a different design?
   There are millions of them too, so how can that be?
A quiet night with snow silently falling from the sky.
   It falls only one flake at a time, so how is it
   that inch upon inch it can come out of nowhere?
Only God knows.

~ 36 ~
Popsicles Can Have Names

Melissa Henderson

"What color do you choose this time?" After eating a healthy lunch of peanut butter sandwiches, mandarin oranges, and strawberries, our two grandchildren were ready for dessert. After the dishes were cleared from the table, Rowan and Eden ran to the kitchen to pick out a favorite color of popsicle.

Red, orange, and purple ice-cold treats on a stick fill the box from the grocery store. Choosing the favorite flavor means keeping the freezer door open a little bit longer than usual. Sometimes we shiver when the cold air touches our faces.

During this recent dessert time, Rowan looked at me and asked, "Mimi, can you make up a story about popsicles?"

I enjoy creating stories and the children often help me with ideas and add their unique details.

I thought for a few seconds and answered, "Yes, of course. Let me see what these cold treats can do for my imagination. Hmm. What about popsicles that want to go outside? Wonder if they would melt?"

As the three of us sat at the table, I began to weave a tale of an ice-cold popsicle named Orangey Parngey, who became friends with Purplely Swirpely. Of course, these are made-up names. But, the more strange the names and descriptions were in the story, the more five-year-old Rowan and two-year-old Eden laughed. Good belly laughs which shook their whole bodies.

As the kids ate their cold treats, they listened and added comments now and then.

Rowan, eating the orange popsicle, added, "Orangey Parngey wanted to go outside, but he would melt. He asked his friends what he should do."

Eden's response was more laughter. She giggled and I giggled.

Drips from the melting popsicles fell onto the napkins on their placemats as they continued taking small bites of the treats. We learned that eating anything cold too fast will cause a "brain freeze."

"What's next? Should the two popsicles have a friend? Maybe Reddy Beddy?" I asked.

Wiggling in their seats, Rowan continued the story and Eden watched with an eagerness only a toddler can show.

Rowan added that the popsicles would be saved if they got back to the freezer before they began to melt.

As we continued to share our made-up story, I realized we were creating more than just a story. We were creating memories. These special times are some of the most memorable moments in our family. Something as simple as a frozen treat and a story created by Rowan, Eden, and Mimi brought happiness and joy.

After we finished the popsicles, I read the jokes on the sticks. That brought on another creative activity: telling jokes. Some were new and others were familiar. Whether we understood the jokes we told or not, we continued to have fun.

The next time I went to the grocery store, I was sure to have popsicles on my list. After all, we need to be prepared; we never know when there might be another silly story waiting to be told at dessert time.

I will always look forward to special moments shared with Rowan and Eden.

~ 37 ~
Come What May

Vicki H. Moss

Without going too deeply into details of the 2016 election year, let's just leave it at this: I was shocked to think I would live to see the day that college students would need teddy bears, safe spaces, and Play Dough to help heal their disappointment over their political candidate not winning. Nor did I ever think they would roam the streets bashing out car windows and blocking roadways so people couldn't get to hospitals during emergencies. Weren't they concerned about love *and* hate?

And all this drama after shootings in Chattanooga — my hometown — Orlando, San Bernadino, and others where police officers were hunted and gunned down by cold-hearted murderers. Police officers who were husbands. Fathers. The first line of defense when law and order is needed.

We're supposed to be evolving. Moving forward as a society. Instead, the world was upside down with this kind of behavior.

However, 2016 brought good news as well. My daughter became pregnant with my third grandchild. After two baby girls, she hoped for a boy. In fact, that thought must have been on her mind because even before she became pregnant, she had an unusual dream.

She dreamed she was in the hospital and had to be sedated for the delivery and when she woke up, she asked her husband for the news: "Boy or girl?"

"We had a boy! And I named him Howie Adventure!"

"What?" screeched out my daughter. "Howie? Howieeeee! Adventure?"

"Well, I thought Howie would go along with the other "H" names of our girls. And you said having a boy after two girls would be an adventure . . . so . . . ."

My daughter yelled, "Hurry! We have to change the name on the birth certificate. We can't name a child Howie Adventure!"

At least 2016 was good for some amusement.

But right before the election in November, I began having dreams about babies. And not about boys wearing baby blue.

Dreaming about an event before it happens isn't unusual for me. Before my daughter flew home from Denver, Colorado to me to tell me she was pregnant with her first child, my deceased mother visited me in a dream in which she and I had gone to a school in Nashville, Tennessee — a school where my daughter had competed in tennis tournaments in years past. Mother and I were at this school to see a child perform on the school's stage. Approximately four years old, this child had long dark hair. She had her back turned to me, so in the dream, I thought I was seeing my own child when she was that age.

Then as dreams usually go, it changed for crazy. Mother and I were in a Walgreen's that seemed to be attached to the same school. I remember thinking in the dream, "This is strange. Drugstores in schools these days." Then suddenly, racks of hand-knitted baby clothes, all in a variegated color of maroon, dark green, and gold caught my attention. Winter colors. There were beautiful dresses with ruffles down the front and in all different sizes from newborn to 4T.

Boys clothes hung on the next rack. Knitted pants that buttoned onto knitted shirts — all out of the same variegated thread of winter colors. I gravitated back to the girl dresses as I always did when looking at baby clothes because buying for girls was more fun.

Mother never said a word. She simply stood nearby as I examined the intricately knitted ruffles on the gorgeous dresses. Then the dream ended. Mother was gone. I'd had only a couple of dreams about her after she'd passed into the arms of Jesus. And in those two dreams, she never spoke. She was simply there. Observing. As though she watched over my family and me from above.

Imagine my surprise when my daughter called to tell me she was flying home from Denver. Over lunch, she burst out with the good news she was pregnant and constantly ill with nausea. I was happy at first, about a new baby, then saddened. Sad because living so far away, I wouldn't be nearby to be with my daughter to help her. The first year of a child's life is one of so many changes, and I would be missing out.

My next thought was about the dream.

"Now I know what my dream meant," I said. "You're going to have a girl. She'll be born in winter. What's the due date?"

"January. But what makes you think it will be a girl?"

I told her the dream. Winter colors on the ruffled dresses.

Me turning away from the boy clothes, more interested in the girl clothes in the dream.

"But what I can't figure out is why I dreamed — in the same dream — you were about three or four years old and performing on a stage in Nashville at a school where you used to play in tennis tournaments when you were in high school."

When my daughter's father-in-law told us he'd dreamed the baby was a boy — "I've even seen his face"— I thought, *Perhaps I was wrong*. But a couple of months later, when my daughter said she and her husband were transferring back to Nashville, I knew *my* dream would come true. I felt God had allowed Mother to visit me in a dream to comfort me with the news that a new baby girl was to be born.

I also knew Mother had had dreams come true. She dreamed her uncle Jack was killed in action during World War II. Within a few days, the family received the telegram that he'd been killed on the Pacific island of Leyte. Many years later, she lost her car keys, and that night she dreamed where she'd left them: outside on the rock ledge of the house. She must have placed them there after she'd driven home from work and had become distracted when talking outside with Daddy.

So in my family, dreams that come true have been a normal happening. And I was holding onto my dream, though if a Howie Adventure was in the future, that would be fine as well.

Fast forward several months. A granddaughter was born.

She later performed on stage in the same school in Nashville I dreamed about. And this child had long dark hair as in the dream.

I didn't dream about the second grandchild. However,

a painting of three females hung on the bathroom wall in my daughter's home. When I was bathing my grandchild, I happened to look up at the painting and think, *that looks like a mom, and before her are two girls headed for a swim in the ocean.* Suddenly, an overwhelming feeling about the second grandchild washed over me. I told my daughter, "You're having another girl."

I wasn't wrong.

When news of the third pregnancy reached me, I had three dreams over a couple of months. In the first dream, the blanket the child was wrapped in was pink. I knew the baby was also a girl. In the other two dreams, the baby I held was again swaddled in pink. I then saw myself walking on a boat deck, carrying the child while negotiating a ledge that tapered back into the boat's hull. To get to the front of the boat, I had to leap from this point, a distance that wasn't safe. I looked down at the deep, murky water and knew that if I tried to jump to the front, I could fall into the water and the babe might drown. The moment after I had this thought in the dream, I was somehow miraculously placed in the front of the boat. All was safe. All was secure. The dream ended. But what did this dream mean? Was there to be a baby girl accompanied by danger and she would miraculously be saved? I shuddered at the thought of danger but rested assured about a miraculous safety net of some sort for this child who was soon to enter the world.

A couple of weeks later, during a gender reveal we learned this third grandchild was definitely a girl and not Howie Adventure.

I thought back on my dream. The murky water. The fear. The devil can't know our thoughts, but he can plant doubt and throw darts to worry us via our dreams. During this questionable moment in time, I declared, "Get behind me Satan. I am protected by the blood of Jesus." I was determined to trust in the Lord for all things. Even faced with something murky and dark on the horizon, I would hold onto faith that God would see my family and me through that darkness.

This third child was another C-section baby. The third girl in the bathroom painting. The girl in the painting I had thought was a mom, seemed now to be the eldest daughter. My daughter's family would be complete with three daughters.

However, it seemed like forever before I received word about the delivery — the surgery had been excruciating and there had been a problem. Could this have been the danger I'd perceived in my dream concerning this child? Or, perhaps the danger would manifest in a future event? I wasn't certain.

What I am certain of is this: *God is our refuge and strength, a very present help in trouble* (Psalm 46:1 KJV). And throughout life, there will always be adventures. Some adventures will be fun. Other adventures like shootings and horrific events around the world will be times of struggling through dark, murky water. The Bible calls these dark adventures trials and tribulations. Yet, come what may, my eyes will forever be on the One — the Light — who has the power to protect and save.

~ 38 ~
Abiding

Nanette Thorsen-Snipes

The young woman stood near the wall, a cane draped over her arm. The pallor of her face, even her whole body was a yellowish tinge. As a member of a newly-established church, I walked over to greet her. Her hands were cold, and it was evident that she didn't feel well.

After that first meeting, I only saw Renita one more time; it was evident that the kidney disease that stalked her was winning.

My heart broke for this young woman in her twenties, and I wanted to do something to ease her suffering. Others took food to her, but I wanted to give food that wouldn't perish. I took her a poem from a small book I had written. Though it hadn't been written specifically for her, I prayed it would touch her.

Several months passed, and my chaotic life with a husband and four children went on. Early one Sunday, her mother, who I had learned was also a member of our church, stopped me before the services began. Smiling broadly, she said, "Every time I go see Renita, she has your poem right by her bed."

I thanked God for using me to bring joy to one of His children, but when we left that church and returned to our former church, I no longer thought about Renita.

I continued sharing my poems with others who were ill or had lost loved ones.

Years passed, and our lives became centered on our children and their activities. As time permitted, I began matting my poems and giving them away.

One day, while my friend Barbara helped me print off my poetry, she received a phone call.

"Oh," I heard her say, "I am so sorry. I didn't know she was that sick . . . ." Barbara's voice trailed off. When she hung up, she looked shocked. "My good friend just died from kidney disease."

I guess the Lord prompted me to ask what her name was.

Barbara simply responded, "Renita."

After learning of this seeming coincidence, Barbara asked if I wanted to go to Renita's memorial service. I declined, since I really didn't know Renita or her family that well.

Later, following the service, I received a phone message from Barbara. "Nan, you won't believe what happened . . . ." She paused a long, awkward moment. "They read your poem at the service."

My heart slowed as I thought about it. Years before, I had offered a ray of hope to a young woman who was dying. And, in turn, she uplifted others. Isn't this what Jesus did?

To me, the rippling effect of that poem is reminiscent of a pebble dropped into a pond, reaching the farthest heart.

Abiding

I feel like the rose, Lord,
After the blush of spring
Has left the petals,
Turned them brown —
Wilted.

The petals are torn away
One by one,
Like pieces of my life,
Drifting aimlessly
On the wind.

I pray for the ability
To pull the rose
Back together
Into a tiny bud —
To begin again.

Day by day, I'll see
The bud open,
Spread its petals,
Kiss the sunshine
And the dew.

In Your gentle hands,
Lord, I'll be that rose
On the vine called love,
And I'll abide in You,
And You in me.

"I am the true vine, and my Father is the husbandman."
John 15:1 KJV

~ 39 ~

Goin' ta Jesus

Mary Anne Quinn

"Let the little children come to me, and do not hinder them, for the kingdom of heaven belongs to such as these."

Matthew 19:14

Bubbles. *That's just what we need here,* I concluded as I studied my new, three-year-old friend. "My name's Alianna," she declared with a pirouette, displaying the flair of both her skirt and her personality. Definitely a bubbles kind of girl.

Her mom and grandfather had come to collect the dining room set my husband and I were donating to a local ministry. As I watched the grown-ups weaving around Alianna, carrying chairs twice her size, I decided she needed an out-of-the-way place that was safe and fun. I snagged two bottles of bubbles from our front closet and led her outside. Bubbles danced with our laughter on a soft breeze before popping on the grass, bushes, and each other. Then I noticed one that just kept floating up. "Look, Alianna!" I exclaimed. "That bubble is going to Jesus."

As Alianna tracked the rising bubble with widening eyes, she made a joyful little bounce and rose up on her tippy-toes as if she might just float up to heaven with it. "Goin' ta Jesus!" she echoed, clapping her hands together with excitement.

At the same moment, a weight of guilt sent my heart sinking. *Why did I just say that? That bubble isn't really going up to Jesus; we're going to see it pop any second. I've just set her up for disappointment.*

Except, it didn't pop. Together we watched the bubble continue to float up and out of our sight. *Jesus loves children, so he must love bubbles.* An image spontaneously formed in my mind of Jesus lounging on His throne, a bottle of bubbles in one hand and a pink plastic wand in the other. He was blowing bubbles, too, iridescent spheres that morphed into hearts as they drifted gently down upon us.

Jesus' broad grin radiated His delight in joining our fun. I sensed Him speak to my heart, "I like being with the kind of little girl who twirls when she tells you her name, and also the kind of woman who keeps bottles of bubbles in her closet. I'm that kind of God."

I knew Alianna's family taught her Jesus loves her, just as they cherished her themselves. With her buoyant personality, I could easily imagine her catching a ride on that bubble all the way to heaven and then running without hesitation right into Jesus' lap. I envied her carefree approach to life because I knew it came from the security of being protected, as well as loved, by the big people in her life.

Jesus' invitation to become like a child has often felt more threatening to me than appealing. I was once a girl who liked to twirl, too. And I was loved, but there weren't any big people in my life who protected me, while there were many who violated my innocence. Being little meant being easy prey. Why would I ever want to be that vulnerable again? Now that I was an adult, a "big person" myself, all I wanted was to be safe.

Jesus wanted to set me free.

Like the disciples who tried to shoo the little children away from Jesus, shame and fear had barred my heart from "goin' ta Jesus" with the same light-hearted spirit as Alianna. But the day Jesus showered me with bubbles and I bathed in His delight, I began a journey of learning to trust in a love that does no harm, discovering that affection need not be synonymous with violation. I still get scared at times, and I close off my heart again, but Jesus remains patient and gentle with me. It is safe to be small and vulnerable with a great big God to take care of me.

Now when I read or hear Jesus' words to "let the little children come to me," I am free to run right into His arms. Just as I laughed and played with Alianna, I am also learning to laugh and have fun with Jesus. I am skipping forward with increasing child-like freedom — with one hand holding onto Jesus, the other holding a pink plastic wand.

~ 40 ~
At the Restaurant

Tim O'Keefe

I'm by myself in a crowded place. It's perfect for people watching. There are so many interesting faces, clothes, hair, and accents.

It's Friday night at large outdoor mall so the place is hopping. A great many people mill around, laughing, teasing, flirting. I'm seated inside a busy restaurant next to the window, my notebook open.

It's warm for the first time in months. Earlier this week it was so cold we had to take plants inside so they wouldn't freeze. Now it's balmy. There's a warm late-afternoon breeze, one of the first true harbingers of spring.

In this hour before sunset the reddish orange glow makes people look beautiful. Most folks just seem happier. It'll get cold again, we know it, but for now it's the perfect time to get outside, celebrate the weather, enjoy the end of the week, go to the mall.

Girls are wearing low risers. (Is that the term? We used to call them hip huggers.) Young guys swagger with sagging pants, their hands reaching back to hoist them up like windshield wipers set on Intermittent. Young families pass by with kids in tow and babies in strollers. Military men and women wear their camouflage fatigues. I guess they haven't had a chance to change from their work clothes. They're not camouflaged very well here.

Two young African American teens with beautiful braids and twists walk by. Those two care about hair. Best friends sharing secrets. Beaming.

A mom and daughter stroll arm in arm wearing matching cutoffs, probably for the first time in months. Their legs are pale. The young girl, maybe twelve, has almost-white-blond hair, long and straight. Her eyes are bright blue. Mom's eyes are the exact same color. You can tell her hair used to be the same blond. They make each other laugh. Then they tilt their heads together and the mom suddenly looks about twenty years younger.

The next pair approaching has been arguing, I think. She's crying. Her head is down; blackish-red hair hides her face. Her shoulders are slumped and her arms are crossed over her chest. There's a name tattooed on her sleeveless tricep: *Adam*. Adam (I presume) looks nonchalant, like he doesn't have a care in the world. The young woman says something I can't hear. He answers. I can't hear him either; they're on the other side of the glass. But I can read his lips easily. It isn't pretty, what he says. They walk on by, her torn tennis shoes in a sad, shuffling gait.

An elderly couple walks into the restaurant slowly and carefully. Holding hands, they approach the booth next to mine. I'm not eavesdropping but I can hear because they're so close.

"You always like a booth," he says.

"And you always let me have the booth," she replies. "Thank you, dear." Her voice is so soft, so southern.

I wonder, *How many times have they said that?* They are old. Eightyish, maybe older. The woman has applied blusher, and lipstick, and eye shadow. She's lovely. She has an obvious limp, maybe a bum hip. She moves into the booth gingerly. Her man helps her as much as he can. And he is gentle. So gentle. He scoots into the booth across from her. Their eyes shine for each other. They set the little pager on the table between them, the one that buzzes and lights up when their order is ready.

It strikes me that this beautiful woman looks a lot like my Heidi — at least the way Heidi might look in twenty years. This woman has had her hair dyed —Heidi probably won't do that — but her eyes are clear, and she has that kind of natural beauty that one doesn't outgrow. She has a beautiful presence as well.

She doesn't just look at her man when they talk; she looks into him. I know that look. I'm in love with it. I have been for over forty years.

Their table buzzer startles them. He slides over to the edge of the booth and stands up slowly, a little creakily. He makes two trips and when he returns with their food trays, he slides back in. They get everything adjusted in front of them, drinks, cutlery, sandwiches, napkins.

Automatically, as if they have done this a million times, they reach their hands across the table and lace fingers then bow their heads and close their eyes. They sigh identical, long sighs. I think, *How many times have they sighed that sigh?*

The man says, "Lord, we thank thee for this day you have made. Bless this food to the nourishment of our bodies and our souls. Lord, let us pause before we eat and think of those in need of food, and shelter, and love." Pause. "And Lord thank you so much for the love of this beautiful woman."

Eyes closed, they smile. Not so much at each other now. They're smiling at God. And now I wonder, *How many times have they thanked God for each other?* Then they unlace their hands and look at each other with love. Quietly, slowly they begin to eat.

I realize I forgot to bless my own food. Hey, I am alone in a restaurant, a public place. Then I close my eyes, and sigh, and I take a moment to give thanks once again for my Heidi. And I am grateful for that little moment. After a hectic day, a long week, I know it wasn't just chance that led me to sit at that table, in that restaurant, with my notebook and eyes open.

I am grateful.

I get up and bus my table and look back at the couple before leaving. They have eyes only for each other.

It is so sweet, so God.

~ 41 ~
Nutting

Janet Faye Mueller

This morning one lone, black squirrel is attempting to eat and store all the hickory nuts from the tree in our backyard . . . yes, all by himself. He's a hard worker and a fast eater.

Seeing all the empty husks on the ground, I am taken back to when I was a child and our family foraged hickory nuts and black walnuts from a friend's grove. Closing my eyes, I can still smell the pungent aroma of black walnuts and the earthy-smelling leaves as we kicked them up from the ground. I hear our laughter and raucous shouts as we kids jumped the small stream that ran through the tree-dotted hills. Sometimes, we didn't quite make it, and our shoes and socks soaked up the cold water. I feel the sun breaking through the clouds, temporarily warming our chilly arms and legs.

Tired and damp from the wet leaves, we head home to store our bounty in the basement. Later, we would spend hours down there, cracking the nuts open and meticulously picking out the coveted meats while tossing out any squiggly worms with disgust.

These precious nut "jewels" later found their way into cookies and fudge for the holiday season. English walnuts do not compare with black walnuts in depth of flavor! As a child, I had no idea that black walnuts contain tannins, a class of substances with antioxidant and anti-inflammatory properties. Little would I have cared then, but now, I love to hear of their health benefits.

Foraging is an art that can be naturally shared with children. It seems to be making a comeback as families are looking for ways to not only save on soaring food prices but also increase the quality of their time spent together.

Nutting is a great way to start the practice of foraging, and the time spent together creates treasured memories.

~ 42 ~
The Well-Watered Plant

Lin Daniels

My best friend, Bev, lived two thousand miles away and was recovering from back surgery. As I contemplated a visit, I felt this strong notion, "If you are going to see her, *now* is the time!" It was an unusual prompt, not filled with anxiety or fear. Not like she was going to die, so I'd better hustle out there to be with her one last time. More like a sense of timeliness. So, I traveled from Hartford to Dallas.

Little did I (or the rest of the world) know that COVID would soon strike.

While at Bev's house, in an effort to be helpful, I asked if there was anything I could do for her. Since she was using a cane and walker to get around, she suggested I water the indoor plants. Although I knew nothing about plants, I was happy to oblige!

As I moved from one plant to another, I came upon a most unusual one. Its flowers were different than any I could remember. And the leaves were an odd texture and hue. It did not seem to absorb the water well, so thinking, *Surely it must be thirsty*, I drenched it some more!

Proud upon completing my assignment, I mentioned to Bev, "What a strange plant!"

She smiled and replied, "Oh, that one's fake. It's made out of plastic."

Meanwhile, my well-intentioned water was overflowing the pot!

At least Bev and I were able to chuckle at the growing puddle on the floor!

Although I did other jobs around her house, watering the fake plant was the most memorable!

~ 43 ~
You've Been Here a Long Time

Melissa Henderson

Our grandchildren, Rowan and Eden, bring laughter into life every day. Activities with the two children include searching for colorful missing toys and finding them hidden at the bottom of the laundry hamper, washing ceramic squirrels and rabbits in the bathtub, hearing about school friends, and making body sounds with armpits. Those young ones bring giggles and joy. Every moment is filled with possibilities and wonder.

Recently, six-year-old Rowan and I were sharing a conversation while he was visiting after school. Rowan began asking about his cousins and other people in the family. We chatted about the ages of different people. His sister Eden is almost three years old.

Friends at his school are about the same age as Rowan. Several birthdays were being celebrated during the month and the topic of age was evident by his questions.

"Mimi, my cousins are old because they are teenagers, right?" The quizzical look on his face showed that his thought process and imagination were trying to register the differences between old and young.

As our chat continued, Rowan paused and looked at me. Cupping my cheeks in his hands, he stared intently into my eyes. Then, he spoke words that made me smile.

"Mimi, you've been on this earth a long time. Are you old?"

"Well, Rowan. My Mama always said that a person wasn't old until they turned one hundred. So, I've got a ways to go. No, I'm not old."

Once again, he paused before speaking. "That's okay, Mimi. Is your back old? Sometimes you can't pick me and Eden up off the ground because you will hurt."

Ah . . . yes, the innocence of a six-year-old. "Yes, sometimes Mimi's back hurts. Not because I'm old. I have some bone aches."

That answer satisfied Rowan. He reached around and gave me a soft pat on the back. His compassion and love were shining through in each tap he gently applied.

Thinking the discussion about age and time was over, I changed the subject and asked if he would like something to eat. A few minutes later, my husband walked into the living room where Rowan and I sat on the couch reading a book and eating fruit snacks.

Rowan noticed Bop and asked the question. "Bop, you've been on this earth longer than me. Are you old?"

Once again, we began discussing the ages of friends, family, and people we see in the neighborhood.

Some of the most precious times are sharing talks with grandchildren. Sometimes they tell what is on their mind and the world becomes a brighter place because of their thoughts and laughter.

Time can move at a quick pace. When we slow our words and actions, take deep breaths, and stay alert for the ways God sends joy, we can shine the light and love of God to others.

As my Mama always said, "You're not old until you reach one hundred". . . even if you've been here a long time.

~ 44 ~

Dear Denise

(A Father's Letter to His Daughter 45 Years Ago)

Robert B. Robeson

As my pen scribbles across this page, 3 A.M. on that special Wednesday morning a little over five years ago refocuses in my mind. It's like recalling the events of a pleasant dream. When the doctor brought you to me at our military hospital in Landstuhl, Germany, I experienced an emotional awakening that undoubtedly encompasses every new father for the first time.

Adult memories enjoy floating amid such reminiscences.

Remember that little Vietnamese baby I told you about recently? She was born on my medical evacuation helicopter in Southeast Asia in May 1970. I told you how close my entire flight crew felt about having been a part of her birth. Well, my feelings were much different with you — because you were "mine." I'll never forget your head sprouting a dark crop of hair, your sleek little face — a few minutes old, peacefully relaxed and looking at me as though you understood everything that was going on.

A wave of tenderness beyond description welled up within me.

In the past five-plus years, I've learned more about the meaning of fatherhood. This knowledge wasn't garnered from a book, TV, or my college professors, but from actually being a father with all of the associated emotions, joys, and sorrows that come with this endeavor. Time has passed swiftly and you're already in school. At this particular moment, I fancy God looking down and saying to me, "Okay, Robeson, I told you I was only lending Denise to you for twenty or so years. Five of them are already gone. Are you doing the best you can with her?" He's quite aware that sometimes I feel as though I've fumbled more than my share of balls that early parenthood has flung at me.

Being a principle party responsible for your birthday has given me a fierce pride and determination to provide a home, food, clothing, and schooling for you. It's also our parental duty and responsibility to take you to church and to train you in the ways of God and love. All of this has demonstrated a very important lesson to me. *Becoming* a father is easy. *Being* a father is the difficult part.

I've been deeply moved by the enormity of the task before us: our having to raise you and you having to put up with us.

When your mother and I became parents, we didn't get divine inspiration telling us how to raise a child. All we've done is the best we know how. And the best we know how is to treat you as much like a human being as possible, and as little like a slave or robot. For some adults, Denise, that's often hard to do. We're not the big experts and we never will be.

Oh, yes, you've shown periods of temperamental behavior much like myself as a youngster (which I believe must have been a subject of constant prayer for your Grandpa and Grandma Robeson). But soon you'll grow wise and begin to comprehend what life is really about.

Since I'm also a soldier, there may be times when you'll have to share me with a part of life no normal individual wishes for. But being a good soldier is much like being a good father. You learn to accept difficulties, lonely roads full of pitfalls, terrors, and other perils far more numerous than I care to mention here. Good soldiers resemble turtles: hard on the outside and soft on the inside. I believe this is the way with most good parents, too, although hardness may seem to appear more often. It's just that we're attempting to teach you not to make some of the dumb mistakes that we've already made.

I know I sometimes display a bit of the neverending-sermon manner. But maybe that's because your Grandpa Robeson and his brother are ministers and my only sibling — your uncle — is a missionary.

What can you do about our inexperience? Probably nothing. Merely attempting to understand in the future will help a lot. That's another dilemma with being a parent. By the time we figure out what we're doing in this position, we become unemployed.

We want you to live your own life and listen to the language of your own heart. But we hope that conversation would always be mindful of God's love and devotion to you.

It's your sacred right to choose your own destiny and realize your own potential. We want you to find the best path for your life and to find your own way at your own pace. And don't worry about or dwell too much on what's ahead. Just go as far as you can. From there, God will allow you to see farther.

It's sad that some men are so busy climbing the ladder of success that they've lost sight of the fact they're also fathers. I don't want that to happen to me. A family without joy, love, or spiritual commitment is like having a favorite puppy die. That's always sad. One of the most important things a father can do for his child is to love its mother. I love yours very much, but it could never be as much as she deserves.

There are also many things I wish could have been. I wish your mother's daddy had lived long enough to have met you. I know he'd have been as proud of you as we are.

Because of your present age, you won't understand a lot of what I've written until you're a lot older. Yet I want to write about it now, as best I can, should something happen and the opportunity escape me.

It's always important to read between the lines, too, like you will with a love letter when you're older. Between the lines is where additional messages and meaning can often be found.

Denise, you're our precious cargo in life. I pray that God will help us guide you to womanhood and that He allows us the luxury and opportunity of living long enough to see you reach it. We both love you very much.

All my love,

Dad

~ 45 ~
Porches and Swings, and Treasured Moments

Terri Kalfas

This morning I sit in the shade of my patio swing's canopy as I drink hot chai and read. It has been too warm to do that most of our Oklahoma summer, but today the soft breeze keeps the morning cool for a while. The same breeze carries the scents of fresh-cut grass wet with morning dew and wood burned last night in someone's firepit. Water in the fountain splashes from bowl to bowl — a pleasant, calming sound, especially when accompanied by the morning bird songs. Cicadas in the willow tree next door occasionally drum their songs, but it's late summer, so their numbers are few now and they no longer drown out the music the neighbor across the street plays as he works out in his garage.

The rumble of planes flying low overhead as they leave the metro for somewhere else, the rhythm of the blades on a life-flight helicopter as it rushes a patient to a hospital a few miles from our home, sirens from fire engines and an ambulance leaving the station near the turnpike entrance a half-mile away, and the steady thrum of cars and motorcycles on that same turnpike — all have become common background noise.

The sounds of our suburban metropolitan area have changed dramatically over the years as this once-small "bedroom city" of Tulsa has grown to become, in its own right, one of the largest cities in the state. They're very different than the pumping oil wells and mournful train whistles of the small oil-town where I grew up.

Its interesting how one thing leads the mind to another, then another. For some reason, today all of these sounds and scents remind me of two very different times and places in my life.

First, the times in my childhood when I sat in the swing that hung on my dad's parents' front porch. Theirs was a tiny home built in 1909 in another small town far from big cities. There, I never heard the thrum of traffic, the rumble of planes and helicopters, or emergency vehicle sirens. Other than Grandma's cooking, I don't recall specific smells. But I do remember that their front porch swing was my favorite place to sit and read, and think, and dream.

Today, the sound of aircraft, and sirens, and turnpike traffic also bring to mind the hours I spent as a young wife and mother sitting at a small table on the front porch of my in-laws's house in New York City. The deep porch extended across the entire front of that house. My husband and his father added it to their home while my husband was in high school. The table, tucked in the corner under a narrow awning and sheltered on two sides by yews, was the perfect spot for reading, and thinking, and praying, and dreaming of the future while people strolled to and from the nearby shops on Union Turnpike, a couple of blocks away.

The morning breeze there was never as strong as what we usually experience here, yet the air always held the distinct aroma of fresh-baked bagels from the shop a few blocks away, mixed with diesel fumes left behind by trucks and city buses as they traveled up and down the busy roadway.

That house sits on LaGuardia's flight path, so many days the frequent roar of jets' engines as they flew low overhead momentarily drowned out other sounds; even conversation stopped until the planes had passed.

It all seems like yesterday.

It also seems so long ago.

We haven't visited New York in several years now. My husband's parents are gone — his father remained in the house with family until Alzheimer's claimed not only his mind but also his life, while his mother lived here with us for over a decade until her death at age one hundred.

My parents are no longer with us, either. Complications from Myasthenia Gravis took my mom; my dad's heart just wore out.

My husband and I don't see our siblings much anymore. We're scattered across the country, and with the deaths of our parents, the magnets that drew us together on holidays and summer vacation, are gone.

Now, I'm my family's matriarch . . . the oldest child of my parents . . . the mother of adult sons . . . the mother-in-law . . . the Yiayia . . . .

So, today, as I sit on my patio swing I think about how I'm in such a different place, not only in location, but also in life. And I think about how, no matter the season of life, there are so very many moments to treasure, especially if we will take each day one moment at a time.

I'm thankful our families have had many. Oh, so many!

Front porches on homes in new neighborhoods seem tiny. Ours is only big enough to hold a planter and one or two people as they enter the house. But we have the patio, where three covered swings are arranged to create a cozy, secluded area on one end.

Some might think three swings are a bit much, but I love it.

The grandchildren think it's a wonderful place, too. When we sit in our swings we plan our next cooking projects and "adventures." We discuss our Christian faith. We talk about other things that are important to them. And sometimes, we pray.

It's a wonderful thing to have memories we treasure. It's also a wonderful thing to be able to create moments for future generations to treasure . . . because treasured moments are an important part of life.

About the Authors

Lisa Braxton is the author of the novel *The Talking Drum*, winner of a 2021 Independent Publisher (IPPY) Book Awards Gold Medal, overall winner of Shelf Unbound Book Review magazine's 2020 Independently Published Book Award, winner of a 2020 Outstanding Literary Award from the National Association of Black Journalists, and a Finalist for the International Book Awards. The Emmy-nominated former television journalist is also an an essayist, and short story writer. She serves on the executive board of the Writers Room of Boston and teaches writing at Grub Street Boston.

Vera Brennan, born in Louisiana and now a resident of upstate New York, loves to tell about her many adventures. She made four trips to Israel: the first living a year in a kibbutz during the Yom Kippur War, the second spending hours in the attic of Christ Church, Jerusalem, copying from original sources about its existence, and the last two as a family helper in the Galilee. When she returned to the U.S., she ended up in a Messianic community in northern Minnesota. From there she was sent to Brooklyn, New York, eventually working as a secretary in Manhattan — a whole new adventure for a small-town Southern girl. Finally came her move to Kingston, New York, where "The Birthing Story" takes place, as well as her marriage to Paul Brennan. (That's another story she loves to tell.) Today, she and Paul are active in their church and enjoy coming along side fellow believers in the Philippines and Mexico.

Ben Cooper is a Christian, husband, father, author, speaker, beekeeper, and more. Growing up on a family farm, getting an Agricultural Science degree from Penn State University, working 32 years for Maryland Department of Agriculture, and being a beekeeper has allowed him to spend much of his time around animals and nature. He uses those experiences as the basis for writing his books and writing for Guideposts' *All God's Creatures*. He resides in the foot slopes of the eastern Continental Divide in southern Pennsylvania. You can contact him at cooperville@breezeline.net.

Lin Daniels retired in 2016 after 39 years of teaching physical education, mostly at the elementary school level. Since then, she has enjoyed writing, preaching on occasion, and working with the youth group at church.

An avid golfer, she and her twin sister play several days a week. They especially delight in playing as partners and dressing almost identically except for one small item (maybe a different color hat). After all, their opponents need to be able to tell them apart as they "zig and zag" a bit as teammates. Recently, Lin has found a passion for pickle ball.

Lin gives thanks to God for the depths of His love as well as all the surprises He has graciously bestowed on her.

Lola De Maci is a retired teacher whose stories have appeared in numerous editions of *Chicken Soup for the Soul, Divine Moments, Guideposts, Reminisce, Los Angeles Times,* and various children's publications and newspaper columns. Lola has a Master of Arts in Education and English, and a Doctorate in Education. She writes overlooking California's San Bernardino Mountains.

Diana Derringer is an award-winning writer and author of *Beyond Bethlehem and Calvary: 12 Dramas for Christmas, Easter,* *and More!* Her articles, devotions, dramas, planning guides, Bible studies, and poems have been accepted more than 1,000 times by 70-plus publications including *The Upper Room, The Secret Place, Clubhouse, Kentucky Monthly, Country, Missions Mosaic,* and several anthologies. She also writes radio drama for Christ to the World Ministries. Her adventures as a social worker, adjunct professor, youth Sunday school teacher, and friendship family for international university students supply a constant flow of writing ideas. You can connect with her on her website — dianaderringer.com — and on Facebook, Twitter, LinkedIn, Instagram, Goodreads, Pinterest, and her Amazon page.

Tanja Dufrene's purpose in writing is to stimulate readers to wholesome thinking (2 Peter 3:1). While leading a ladies group, she recognized the sincerity of many Christ followers, but was concerned about their lack of biblical knowledge. So, she began writing weekly devotional emails, hoping to inspire her readers to draw closer to God. Some of those writings are found in *Artesian Zeal*, her first devotional book. Another ladies' Bible study resulted in the *Warrior of the Word* series. Both are available through Amazon and Barnes & Noble. She shares a daily minute devotional on her *Warrior of the Word* Facebook page. Tanja became an ordained minister in 2011. You can follow her on LinkedIn, Twitter, Instagram, Pinterest and her website www.WarrioroftheWord.faith, or contact her via email at WarrioroftheWord@yahoo.com.

Terri Elders, a licensed clinical social worker and lifelong writer and editor, has contributed to nearly 150 anthologies, including multiple editions of *Chicken Soup for the Soul*. She writes feature articles and travel pieces for regional, national, and international publications. Terri lives in her native southern

California, not far from her beloved Pacific Ocean. She can be "friended" on Facebook.

Carol Graham is a charismatic master storyteller whose message is passionate and uplifting. With riveting true stories, Carol conveys how to overcome doubt, fear, trauma, and everything in between. She is an expert in surviving against all odds.

Carol received the Woman of Impact Award and Author of the Year for her memoir, *Battered Hope,* and the global award for *One Woman – Fearless* given to women who have faced their fears and made the world a better place for women to thrive.

The award-winning author is also a keynote speaker, prayer coach, teacher, podcaster, YouTuber, and dog rescuer.

Lydia E. Harris has been married to her college sweetheart, Milt, for more than 50 years. She enjoys spending time with her family, which includes two married children and five grandchildren.

She is the author of three books for grandparents: *Preparing My Heart for Grandparenting: for Grandparents at Any Stage of the Journey, In the Kitchen with Grandma: Stirring Up Tasty Memories Together,* and the newly released *GRAND Moments: Devotions Inspired by Grandkids.*

With a master's degree in Home Economics, Lydia creates and tests recipes with her grandchildren for Focus on the Family children's magazines. She also pens the column "A Cup of Tea with Lydia," which is published in the U.S. and Canada. It's no wonder she is known as "Grandma Tea."

Melissa Henderson, an award-winning author, hopes to encourage readers with inspirational messages sometimes laced with a bit of humor. With stories online and in print publications, Melissa is the author of "Licky the Lizard" and "Grumpy the Gator." An Elder, Deacon and Stephen Minister, her passions are helping in the community and church. Follow Melissa on Facebook, Twitter, Pinterest, Instagram, Goodreads, Bookbub, Youtube, Linkedin, and at http://www.melissaghenderson.com.

Helen L. Hoover and her husband of 60 years are retired and live in the Ozark Mountains of south-central Missouri. Sewing, reading, knitting, tending the flower and veggie gardens, and helping her husband with home repair occupy her time now. Word Aflame Publishing, *The Secret Place*, Word Action Publication, *The Quiet Hour*, *The Lutheran Digest*, Light and Life Communications, *Chicken Soup for the Soul*, and Victory in Grace have published her devotionals and personal articles. Helen and her husband treasure visits with their two living children, and their grandchildren and great-grandchildren.

Charles Huff has served as Bible teacher and minister in his church for twenty years. His devotions have appeared in www.christiandevotions.us, *The Upper Room*, and InspireAFire.com. He has articles in three anthologies: *Gifts from Heaven: True Stories of Miraculous Answers to Prayer*; *Short and Sweet Too*, and *Short and Sweet Takes the Fifth*. His book *Victim No More: How Forgiving Dad Turned Victim to Victor* was published in February 2023. He is a member of Word Weavers International and serves as a president of a Word Weavers On-line Critique Group. Connect with him at: www.chashuff.wordpress.com, and www.charlesjhuff.com.

Terri Kalfas loves working with words. She began her career in journalism as student-government reporter and managing editor of *The Daily O'Collegian*, the Oklahoma State University student newspaper. Before taking a break to be home with her children, she worked as a reporter, freelancer, and editor for various other newspapers. Terri has worked in the Christian publishing industry since 1987, holding positions ranging from editor to publisher, and teaching at writers conferences across the U.S. and Canada. She and her husband, George, have three sons, two daughters-in-law, and six grandchildren with whom they love spending time.

Bob LaForge has been a Christian since 1977. He and his wife, Toni, have twin daughters, Sarah and Danielle, who were born in 2006. The family attends Grace Bible Church where Bob oversees the bookstore and teaches Adult Sunday School.

Bob has over 300 publications and has written four books which are available from Amazon. Three are nonfiction: *Contemplating the Almighty*, which discusses who and what God is, *Developing Great Relationships*, and *The End Times and the Bible*. The fourth, *The Tempter Comes,* is a novel. Church Growth Institute published his "Evaluating Your Friendship Skills." His books as well as articles, devotions, several Bible Study series, and a section on Bible literacy are available to download at no charge at disciplescorner.com. Tracts you can print and distribute are also available there at no charge.

Beverly Hill McKinney has published over 700 inspirational articles in such publications as *Good Old Days, Sharing, Breakthrough Intercessor, Woman Alive, P31* and *Plus Magazine*. She has devotions in *Cup of Comfort Devotional: Daily Reflections of God's Love and Grace, Open Windows, God Still Meets Needs* and *God Still Leads and Guides*. Her stories have been featured in anthologies such as *Christmas Miracles, Men of Honor,* Guidepost's *Extraordinary Answers to Prayer, Additional Christmas Moments, Precious Precocious Moments,* and *Loving Moments*. She has also self-published *Through the Parsonage Window* and *Whispers from God: Poems of Inspiration*. Beverly, who lives in Oregon, graduated from the Jerry B. Jenkins Christian Writer's Guild at both Apprentice and Journeyman levels.

Norma C. Mezoe has been a published writer for 38 years. Her writing has appeared in books, devotionals, Sunday school take-home papers, magazines, and online. She became a Christian at the age of 15, but didn't grow spiritually in a significant way until a crisis at the age of 33 brought her into a closer relationship with the Lord. Her desire is to honor God with her writing, and to encourage and point others to Jesus Christ. Norma can be contacted at: normacm@tds.net.

Vicki H. Moss is former Editor-at-Large and Contributing Editor for *Southern Writers Magazine* where she interviewed authors and contributed articles on writing in addition to blogging for the magazine's *Suite T* blog. She also wrote a weekly column as a pundit for the *American Daily Herald*. As a workshop instructor for writers conferences, Vicki teaches from her books *How to Write for Kids' Magazines* and *Writing With Voice*. With over 750 articles published, she co-authored the book *nailed It!* and contributed to Cecil Murphey's book, *I Believe in Heaven*. When Vicki's not gardening, making author visits, or teaching a class on "Writing the Stories Behind the Recipes," she writes poetry that's published in magazines and her books on writing.

Janet Faye Mueller writes from a small, rural community in northeast Indiana. She has a penchant for drawing spiritual analogies from everyday observations. Devotionals, short stories, "God stories," and poetry provide the perfect outlet for these analogies. Janet founded Heartland Writers Circle, a church-based ministry of creative writers. She is also a Creative Writing Leader for United Adoration, a nonprofit organization whose mission is to revitalize the creativity of the local church. Janet writes a blog, *Views From the Empty Nest*, and has been published in a variety of magazines. She and her husband are celebrating 40 years of marriage. They have two adult sons, a beautiful daughter-in-law, and two adorable grandsons. Janet enjoys woman-talk, good coffee, encouraging encounters, and hearty laughter!

Tim O'Keefe has been married to his best friend for 42 years. He is the father of two young men, who he also considers his best friends. Tim retired after 38 years teaching young children — a job he dearly loved. He has won awards including the National Council of Teachers of English (NCTE) Outstanding Elementary Educator (2014). Tim has written and published extensively for teachers including NCTE's *Looking Closely, Listening Carefully* and Heinemann's *Mathematics in the Making*. Since retiring from teaching, He has completed a novel titled *Falling Forward,* for middle grades, and a novel titled *Blues Lessons and Ben Tillman* for adults.

Mary Anne Quinn lives in the Chicago area with her husband, John. She enjoys biking and birding in the local forest preserves, relaxing at the beach, singing in worship choirs, and putting together jigsaw puzzles while listening to classical music.

Mary Anne's personal experience of emotional healing has equipped her to help others along their journey to a securely-attached relationship with God. Whether she is writing articles and devotions or presenting her signature workshop, *Joyful Identity*, to churches and small groups, Mary Anne's stories always focus on building joy in the living, interactive presence of Jesus. Learn more about Mary Anne and connect with her at creativelyattached.com.

Sue Rice began authoring short stories when she lost her twin sister in 2016 and wrote about the experience. *Guideposts Magazine* published her first story. Since that time, she has been published in several magazines and anthologies. Her letters to the editor have been published in *Epoch Times* and her local newspaper.

Since retiring as an HR Director, Sue has taught ESL for six years and enjoys watching her children and grandchildren become who God meant them to be. She and her husband of 54 years love to travel, spend time with family, and watch the antics of their four-footed "kids" — a dog and a cat. Sue also works with Braver Angels, a nationwide organization whose mission is to heal the divide in our country.

Robert Robeson's 968 articles, short stories and poems have been published in 77 anthologies and 330 publications in 130 countries. This includes the *Reader's Digest, Writer's Digest, Positive Living, Vietnam Combat, Official Karate, Soldier of Fortune* and *Writer's Yearbook 2014*, among others. After retiring as a lieutenant colonel from a 27½-year Army career as a helicopter medical evacuation pilot, Robert served as a newspaper managing editor and columnist. He has a BA from the University of Maryland, College Park and has completed extensive undergraduate and graduate work in journalism at the University of Nebraska, Lincoln. He lives in Lincoln, Nebraska with his wife of 54 years, Phyllis.

Amari Seymour always loved reading and thought it would be cool to become an author when she was older. Now, after graduating college with a minor in creative writing, she is an aspiring author. She is in the process of editing a novella she wrote in her sophomore year of high school, and extending a short story she wrote that same year into a mystery novel. Amari has seven siblings, five older sisters and two younger brothers. She currently resides in La Porte, Indiana with her mom and brothers.

Tammie Edington Shaw has been an editor of a weekly newspaper, a production coordinator for a magazine and a product coordinator for David C. Cook Publishing. Her work has appeared in *Guideposts, LIVE, The Christian Communicator, Pathways to God, God's Word for Today, The Secret Place, Journey,* and the Divine Moments anthology *Christmas Stories.* She was co-compiler and contributor to *Writing So Heaven Will Be Different*. For 15 years she was on the staff of the Write-to-Publish Conference. She and her husband live in Illinois.

Laura Sweeney facilitates Writers for Life in Iowa and Illinois. She represented the Iowa Arts Council at the First International Teaching Artist's Conference in Oslo, Norway. Her poems and prose appear in more than 60 journals and 10 anthologies in the U.S., Canada, Great Britain, Indonesia, and China. Her recent awards include a scholarship to the Sewanee Writer's Conference. In 2021, she received an Editor's Prize in Flash Discourse from *Open: Journal of Arts & Letters,* and the Poetry Society of Michigan's Barbara Sykes Memorial Humor Award. Two of her poems appear in the anthology *Impact: Personal Portraits of Activism,* which received an American Book Fest Best Book Award in its Current Events category, and finalist in the Social Change category. She is a PhD candidate in English/Creative Writing, at Illinois State University.

Annmarie B. Tait resides in Harleysville, Pennsylvania with her husband, Joe Beck, where they are at last embarking on retirement. In addition to writing tales about the memories made growing up in her large, Irish-Catholic family, she also cultivates her passion for, cooking, crocheting, *Scrabble*, and as of late, *Wordle*. She also enjoys singing and recording Irish and American Folk Songs. Annmarie's stories have been published in several volumes of *Patchwork Path, Chicken Soup for the Soul,* the HCI *Ultimate* series, *Reminisce* magazine, and the Blue Mountain Press publication *Irish Inspirations*. Contact Annmarie at: irishbloom@aol.com.

Nanette Thorsen-Snipes, freelance editor, proofreader, and writer in the Christian publishing industry, has been writing much of her life. She has contributed stories and devotions to more than 70 compilation books, the Guideposts *Miracle* series, *Chicken Soup for the Soul, God's Way, Soul Matters, New Women's Devotional Bible*, and *The Cat in the Christmas Tree* among others. She has published over 500 articles and stories, dozens of magazine articles, devotions, children's stories, including reprints, in over 40 print publications. Her stories have been included in five of the previous books in the Divine Moments series. Contact her at nsnipes@bellsouth.net.

If you enjoyed

Treasured Moments

you might also enjoy these
books in the *Divine Moments* Series

Divine Moments
Christmas Moments
Spoken Moments
Precious, Precocious Moments
More Christmas Moments
Stupid Moments
Additional Christmas Moments
Why? Titanic Moments
Loving Moments
Merry Christmas Moments
Cool-inary Moments
Moments with Billy Graham
Personal Titanic Moments
Remembering Christmas
Romantic Moments
Pandemic Moments
Christmas Stories
Broken Moments
Celerating Christmas
Grandma's Cookie Jar
Can, Sir!
Christmas Spirit
Joy to the World
Lost . . . and Found

Grace Publishing Anthologies

If you're a writer with a story to tell, consider submitting your work for inclusion in an upcoming Grace Publishing anthology.

Divine Moments

Divine Moments is an award-winning series. Each book is a labor of love, so no one is compensated monetarily. Authors share with the possibility of changing someone's life, heart, or mind. All royalties from this series go to Samaritan's Purse, an organization that helps victims of war, poverty, natural disasters, disease, and famine with the purpose of sharing God's love through His son, Jesus Christ. However, each of the authors whose work is selected to be published will receive a free copy of the book and a discount on orders.

Send your personal articles! The story is the important thing. The article length is anywhere from 500-2,000 words. Previous books have included poems and even some pieces written by children, so the guidelines aren't strict. The main point is the context of the story. (Take a look at previous Moments books that Grace Publishing has released for examples.)

Both multi-published and beginning or non-published authors write for the series. Stories may be original or previously published if rights have been returned (as long as we are informed of the latter in advance). Grace Publishing retains rights after acceptance until publication, then rights automatically return to the author.

Submissions should be Times New Roman, 12-point type, sent as a Microsoft Word attachment to an email. Subject line should include the title of the book. Please include in the header at the top of the submission: your name, mailing address, email address, phone number, and the story's word count. Also include with your submission a bio of 100-125 words. Each writer's bio will appear in the About the Author section at the end of the book. Send to Terri Kalfas: terri@grace-publishing.com.

Divine Moments Is Accepting Submissions for the Following Titles

Questionable Moments: Whether these stories are serious or funny, they should be the "What was I thinking?" type of story. They might even address whether the questionable behavior was redeemed or even redeemable, and why or why not.

Divine Detours: Stories that show how your personal plans/goals/actions were changed because of God's movement in your life and when or how you realized God was in control and "behind" it all.

Unexpected Kindness: These should be stories of a time in your life when you or someone you know received unexpected or undeserved kindness/help/grace from others.

Patriotic Moments: Stories of actions that exemplify true personal love and celebration of the U.S.

Hopeful Moments: These stories should be uplifting. They can include (but are not limited to) what hope and hopefulness means to you, seasons of hope you have experienced, and stories of times when all hope seemed lost until. . . .

Short and Sweet Series

Each book in the *Short and Sweet* series is a labor of love, so no one is compensated monetarily. Authors share with the possibility of changing someone's life, heart, or mind. All royalties from this series go to World Christian Broadcasting, a non-profit organization whose purpose is to take God's Word — through mass media — to people who may have no other means of hearing the Good News. Each of the authors whose work is selected to be published will receive a free copy of the book and a discount on orders.

For this book series we use words of only one syllable in the stories related to the book's theme.

Seven exceptions to the one-syllable-word-only requirement:

1. Any proper noun is okay. (If you were born in California, don't write Maine; if a name is Machenheimer, don't write Clark.)

2. You may use polysyllabic words of 5 letters or fewer — for example: into, over, area, about.

3. You may use contractions of more than one syllable such as couldn't, wouldn't, didn't.

4. You may use numbers (even those that are polysyllabic).

5. As in any published work, direct quotes — even in casual conversation — must be rendered word-for-word as they occurred, so their wording is exempt from the rules. This includes verses from the Bible — but only translations, not paraphrases (such as *The Message*).

6. Multi-syllable words for family (for which there are no single-syllable synonyms) are fine: mother, father, family, sister, brother, sibling, husband, daughter, relative etc.

7. Words for which no synonym exists — such as college/university, heredity, communication, integrity, honest/honesty, person, regret, career/

profession, passion, destination, hospital, education/ teacher/professor, institution, creativity, identity — or that cannot be replaced by a natural-sounding phrase of simple, one-syllable words.

Writers often find it easier to write the story, then go back and replace the words that don't meet the series' requirements.

The general purpose of your piece is to entertain — rather than to teach or merely inform — so the tone should be personal and optimistic rather than instructive.

Both multi-published and beginning or non-published authors write for the series. Stories may be original or previously published if rights have been returned (as long as we are informed of the latter in advance). Grace Publishing retains rights after acceptance until publication, then rights automatically return to the author.

The article length is anywhere from 250-1,000 words. Previous books have included poems. The main point is the context of the story. (Take a look at previous *Short and Sweet* books that Grace Publishing has released.)

Submissions should be Times New Roman, 12-point type, sent as a Microsoft Word attachment to an email. Subject line should include the title of the book. In the header at the top of the submission, include: your name, mailing address for the one free copy, your email address, phone number, and the story's word count.

Please include with your submission a clear, crisp, 300 ppi/dpi color headshot (as an attachment in jpeg format) and a a bio of no less than 100 and no more than125 words. Each writer's photo and bio will appear in the About the Author section at the end of the book.

Contact Susan King at shortandsweettoo@gmail.com to obtain the upcoming theme deadline or submit your work.

Short and Sweet Is Accepting Submissions for the Following Titles

Growing Older With Grace (and a Little Humor): pieces can range from touching to hilarious. Writers who aren't seniors can write about their observations of friends, family members, and everyday encounters. Beyond just funny situations, topics can focus on the benefits of aging, especially in becoming wiser and more mature. Younger writers can also share what they are learning in the process.

Those Memorable Mutts and Feline in the Family

Facing Fears: Facing and conquering fears big or small, whether as a child or an adult.

www.ingramcontent.com/pod-product-compliance
Lightning Source LLC
Chambersburg PA
CBHW070451100426
42743CB00010B/1579